IN NO TIME

Dreamweaver 4

Susanne Rupp

In No Time

Dreamweaver 4

An Imprint of Pearson Education

PEARSON EDUCATION LIMITED

Head Office:
Edinburgh Gate
Harlow CM20 2JE
Tel: +44 (0)1279 623623
Fax: +44 (0)1270 431059

London Office:
128 Long Acre
London WC2E 9AN
Tel: +44 (0)20 7447 2000
Fax: +44 (0)20 7240 5771
Website: www.it-minds.com

First published in Germany in 2001
© Pearson Education Limited 2002

First published in 2001 as *Easy Dreamweaver 4*
by Markt & Technik Buch-und-Software-Verlag GmbH
Martin-Kollar-Straße 10-12
D-81629 Munich
Germany

This edition published 2002 by Pearson Education

British Library Cataloguing in Publication Data
A CIP catalogue record for this book can be obtained from the British Library.

ISBN 0-130-66006-X

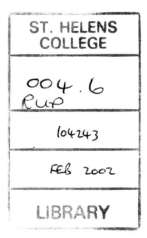
Almost all hardware and software names that are used in this book are
registered trademarks or should be regarded as such.

10   9   8   7   6   5   4   3   2   1

Translated and typeset by Cybertechnics, Sheffield.
Printed and bound in Great Britain by Ashford Colour Press, Gosport, Hampshire.

The Publishers' policy is to use paper manufactured from sustainable forests.

Contents

Chapter 8: Forms   211

Chapter 9: Layers   225

Introduction

A warm welcome from Dreamweaver 4.

Dreamweaver is a very highly efficient WYSIWYG editor (What You See Is What You Get) produced by Macromedia. It will be used by professional Web designers and Web site developers, as well as by beginners who want to build their own Internet or Intranet presence.
Dreamweaver 4 is one of the best editors there has ever been.

With Dreamweaver, you can build professional Web sites without any knowledge of HTML (**H**yper **T**ext **M**arkup **L**anguage). The source code is automatically generated by Dreamweaver.

The development of JavaScript is mere child's play.

On the other hand, you can also directly edit and write in the source code. Therefore, Dreamweaver is a suitable tool for professional Web developers.

You will get much benefit from this book even if you consider yourself to be a beginner. Previous experience is not required. You will find the basics for working with Dreamweaver here. As well as this basic knowledge, the book contains valuable information, tips and stimulus for further development of your Web site.

Everything is well documented.

Each chapter in this book is created and structured as a workshop. It will explain step by step how you can build your own Web site using Dreamweaver 4.

Chapter 1 familiarises you with the basic structure and the philosophy of the program. Here you will find an overview of the opportunities and the terminology used in Dreamweaver.

The main subject in **Chapter 2** is Web site management. You will learn how to keep an overview of your work in Dreamweaver. Whether you can only manage an Internet presence of a few pages, or wish to go on to create a more comprehensive project — this is where you learn how it works. You will then learn how to create content for your Web site.

Chapter 3 is about text and paragraphs. What do you have to take into account if you insert new text, use old documents or modify existing pages? This is where you will also find information on formatting and structuring of text into paragraphs. Here, you will also learn the basics of creating a layout in HTML.

Chapter 4 concentrates on working with images. Liven up your Web site with appropriate photos and graphics. This workshop will show you the issues that must be taken into account.

What would the Internet be without hyperlinks? **Chapter 5** shows you the opportunities hyperlinks offer and how to use them.

Normally, you would use tables for creating a layout in Web sites. In **Chapter 6** you will learn that these do not always need to be visual and you also learn how to get tables right.

Chapter 7 deals with several documents in one browser window, by arranging them in frames. This workshop explains how this works and which alternatives these frames provide to tables.

Naturally, you want to make contact with other people and users through your Internet presence. Whether you are introducing your association or your hobby on the Internet, without some feedback from your Internet visitors your presentation is of little relevance and the exercise will only be half the fun. That's why **Chapter 8** shows you how to create forms and how to get them up and running.

You can quite easily create several layers with Dreamweaver.

In **Chapter 9** you will experience how to arrange objects on top of and underneath each other on a page.

Interactive activity means that you have one or several elements on the Web page which react to the users' actions. In **Chapter 10** you will learn about the options Dreamweaver has to offer.

You can import Flash animations directly in the new Dreamweaver. In **Chapter 11** you can read about how this is done and the other options for integrating further multimedia elements on the Web page.

In the last workshop in **Chapter 12** you will experience how to publish your finished Web site.

Useful tips will help you to get a head start. In the **Appendix** you will find a dictionary of terms as an additional service for beginners, which lists the most important actions, an overview of the most important keyboard commands (shortcuts), and a help chapter that answers questions about problems and offers interesting surfing tips, including information on the most important search engines.

What is new in Dreamweaver 4?

Those of you who already have some experience with Dreamweaver 3 will obviously want to know what is so special about the new version. There are a number of changes, extensions and new features, which are explained in detail in the individual chapters. But let's look at a summary presentation of the most important changes:

In the new Dreamweaver, direct editing of HTML source text is much simplified. To start with, the **Code Editor** is now placed directly in the document window.

Now you can also place and edit **Cascading Style Sheets, JavaScript**, **XML** and other code files directly in the integrated code editor. By using the integrated JavaScript debugger, you can easily see how the browser is able to interpret the code.

Code: Thanks to the integrated **Online reference,** you keep the overview of all HTML functions.

You can produce pure source code with Dreamweaver, which can be converted by both Internet Explorer and Netscape.

Thanks to the characteristic different coloured code elements, you always keep a clear overview of the situation. In doing so, you have complete control over your source code.

In addition, **site management** is optimised and the job sequence is clearly simplified. In this way, Dreamweaver allows effective **teamwork**. You can remain in close contact with the people who work with you and keep a full overview of the work in progress.

Extensive **tests** optimise the source code of your site and thereby prevent unpleasant surprises. Both of the most important browsers, Internet Explorer and Netscape, are catered for.

Now you can create simpler and more efficient **tables** as a basis for your layout.

You can quickly and almost directly develop graphic elements in Dreamweaver. **Flash** and **Fireworks** are very well integrated in Dreamweaver 4.

In addition, there are more possibilities for software **configuration**. You can arrange the windows according to your individual needs, and create your own keyboard shortcuts. Macromedia comes with a default setup, which you can alter, delete and extend at any time.

Working with **windows** and **panels** has also become easier and is more clearly laid out. Macromedia has created a uniform standard with its new software products (Dreamweaver 4, Fireworks 4, Flash 5). You will note that the user interface is almost identical in all programs, which makes working with them considerably easier.

Effective **teamwork** is possible thanks to the efficient integration of tools and systems (such as element management, reporting throughout the site, configurable site windows, integrated e-mail, Extension Manager, Macromedia Exchange, Microsoft Visual SourceSafe, WebDAV). Project management has never been so simple.

Only for Mac users

Dreamweaver 4 is available both for Windows and Macintosh. This book was written for the PC. But the Mac version is very close to it. There are no longer large differences in today's versions.

Sometimes, you will find that the buttons have different names. In many of the Windows dialogue windows, for example, the button is called "BROWSE". On a Mac, these buttons are called "SELECT". Both buttons have the same function.

The browser and its dangers

Currently, Internet Explorer (sometimes called IE, MSIE or Explorer) from Microsoft is the most used browser. It is already available in version 5.5.

Netscape (also Navigator or simply NN) is the second largest browser manufacturer. NN 6 is the most recent version.

There are minor differences in user-friendliness and security, which are negligible. However, the differences in the display of the HTML source code are much more important to Web designers and Web developers.

You should also know a bit about representation (or non representation) of CSS, layers and JavaScript.

You will learn what to take into account in the individual chapters.

Let's get started ...

Now our workshop can begin. At the beginning of every chapter, the aims of the chapter are briefly summarised.

Important terms you should know are explained under WHAT IS THIS? You will find additional information under NOTE. Other technical terms are also described in the dictionary.

TIPS make your work easier.

What you should also look out for is placed under CAUTION.

And so, we can begin...

5

Chapter 1

The beginning

In our first workshop, you will experience everything about the basic construction of Dreamweaver 4. This basic knowledge is useful so that you can find your way around the program quickly and easily. You will then learn the Dreamweaver user terminology step by step.

If you have completed the installation of Dreamweaver and started it for the first time, you will see a split main window and several more floating windows called palettes or inspectors.

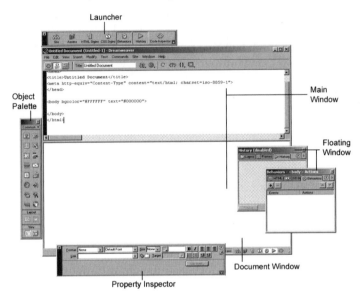

First of all, we will look at the technical language used in Dreamweaver. We will then proceed to try out and practise with what is hidden behind each of the program elements.

The Dreamweaver terminology

Although all the program components are available from the Window menu, not all of them are called windows.

According to the Dreamweaver terminology, windows will appear in the windows status bar. Only the document and the site window in Dreamweaver are stand-alone screen elements.

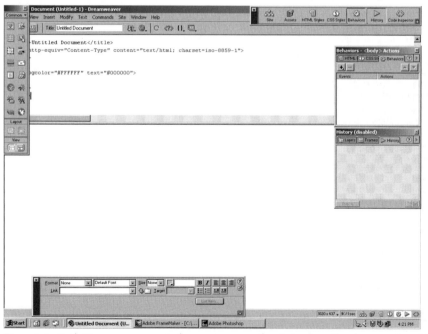

Figure1.1: Both Dreamweaver windows appear on the status bar: the document and the site window

The small floating windows are called panels or inspectors.

If you have ever worked with multimedia development programs, you will know these windows from Director, Photoshop or PageMaker. Fireworks, the program closely tied in with Dreamweaver, also uses these program elements.

The appearance of the inspectors changes according to the selected criteria. For example, the Property Inspector always shows the properties of the currently marked object.

The panels keep control over the whole site. Here, elements such as style and library are managed, which are generally available for the whole site.

> **NOTE**
>
> *Panels and inspectors are actual windows in the true sense of the word. I will use the term window in my description, independent of its characteristics.*

You can move, close and alter the size of each window. Use the well-known Microsoft or Macintosh buttons for this.

You can also close opened windows using the menu bar. Opened windows are checked on the left of the displayed name.

If you want to close the window, simply select the respective name in the window menu. The checking disappears when the window is closed.

> **TIP**
>
> *It could be that a panel or a window is open but does not appear on the screen. Then choose WINDOW/ARRANGE PANELS (see below).*

You can move each of the floating windows back and forth. However, the more floating windows you have opened, the less clear the work space is.

How to arrange the work area:

To arrange the floating objects on the edge of the screen, choose WINDOW/ ARRANGE PANELS.

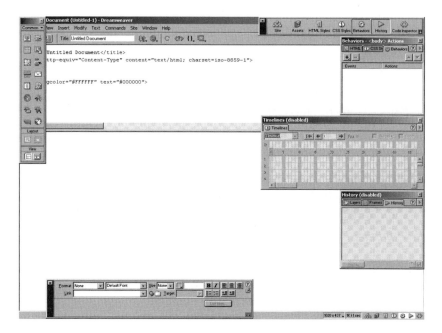

You can hide all of the windows by pressing 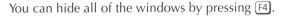.

If you press this key again later, the previously opened windows will reappear in the same place. You can also proceed via WINDOW/ARRANGE/ HIDE PANELS.

Also, if the program is closed down and later restarted, Dreamweaver has the ability to recover the position of the individual windows.

If you work with several programs at the same time, it can be useful to minimise Dreamweaver at times, without having to close it down completely. This is carried out by the commands WINDOW/MINIMISE ALL. The keyboard shortcut for this is: ⇧ + F4. Dreamweaver then disappears and is only present in your status bar, which makes space for other programs and allows you to carry on with your other work.

You can have several Web sites open at the same time. Every file name is shown in the Window menu. You switch between the different files by clicking on the file names. In the following figure, three documents are open.

Opened Documents

If you would like to minimise all the Dreamweaver windows, go to WINDOW/ MINIMISE ALL ($\boxed{\text{Alt}}$ + $\boxed{\Uparrow}$ + $\boxed{\text{F4}}$). Using this command, they will be minimised to floating windows and can easily be arranged as you like. In this way you could for example work on several HTML documents at the same time, without having to switch between the windows.

You can see three floating windows in the following figure.

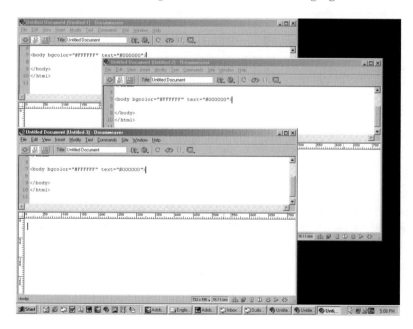

A section describing functions could also be called up using the usual Windows or Macintosh buttons. In Table 1.1 I have listed keyboard shortcuts and menu commands.

▭	WINDOW/MINIMIZE ALL	⇧ + F4	puts all of the Dreamweaver windows in the status bar
▣	WINDOW/RESTORE ALL	Alt + ⇧ + F4	changes maximised Dreamweaver windows into floating and makes it possible to move the document windows
✖	FILE/CLOSE or	Ctrl + W	closes the active document window
	FILE/EXIT	Ctrl + Q	closes all document windows and exits the program

Table 1.1: As usual with individual programs, Dreamweaver integrates the keyboard shortcuts provided by Windows in the menu bar.

CAUTION

If you are about to close the last document window, Dreamweaver will ask if you would like to exit the program.

*If you confirm the "**Don't warn me again**" message, in future the program will be shut down immediately without further warning. Dreamweaver will keep asking this question every time if you do not click the Yes check box.*

It has often happened that, instead of closing only one document, I have unintentionally quit the whole program.

Make yourself familiar with the program first, and check carefully before clicking the box.

The document window

The document window is the core of Dreamweaver. The layout in the document window is very close to what will actually be displayed in a browser. This is why Dreamweaver is also described as a WYSIWYG editor.

WHAT IS THIS?

WYSIWYG: *"What You See Is What You Get"*

WYSIWYG means that what you construct and see in the program will be exactly the same as when viewing it in the Web page. There may, however, be differences in the individual browsers.

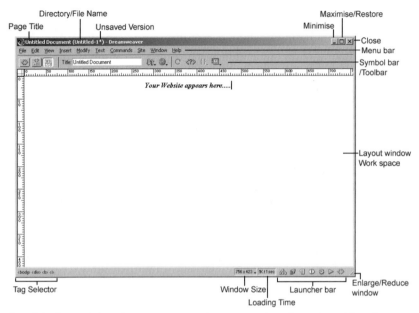

The **title bar** of the document window contains the page title, the name of the directory where the file is saved, and the filename. A star appears behind the filename if the document still has no saved elements.

All Dreamweaver commands are available in the **menu bar**.

The Dreamweaver status bar

The document window below ends with the status bar. Further information about your developed Web page is available here.

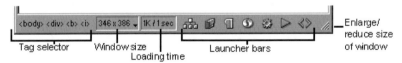

The **Tag Selector** shows the HTML source code of the selected area, where the appearance and the properties of text elements or objects are defined. You can select HTML code quickly using this method.

`<body> <div> <b> <i>`

Click on these tags to select the corresponding content of the document window. If you click on **<body>** you will select the whole work space. You will learn how to work with this in the Selecting objects section on page 29.

WHAT IS THIS?

Tag: You define the appearance of a Web page using these HTML short commands. You can format text, insert images and link pages with the tags.

Normally, tags enclose the document part with the relevant start and end tags.

Examples:

<p></p> inserts a paragraph.

<a href></a> refers to another Internet page or to specified places in the same document or in another document.

<body></body> surrounds the visual content of a document in a browser.

You will learn more about the construction of the page source code in the chapter on the HTML Source Inspector.

You can modify the size of the Dreamweaver windows to specified pixel values in the WINDOW SIZE pop-up menu. By doing so, you will get a clear impression of what the window would look like in different screen sizes and settings.

1 Click on the layout area to be sure that this is the active work space.

Simply click on the WINDOW SIZE pop-up menu:

`760 x 420 ▾`

2 Select the window size you would like.

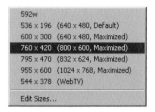

```
592w
536 x 196   (640 x 480, Default)
600 x 300   (640 x 480, Maximized)
760 x 420   (800 x 600, Maximized)
795 x 470   (832 x 624, Maximized)
955 x 600   (1024 x 768, Maximized)
544 x 378   (WebTV)
Edit Sizes...
```

How to change the value in the WINDOW SIZE pop-up menu:

1 Choose EDIT SIZES in the WINDOW SIZE pop-up menu. The PREFERENCES dialog box with the STATUS BAR active panel appears.

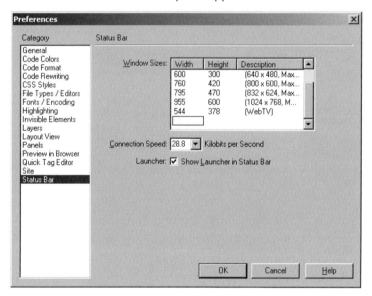

2 The cursor is placed where you can begin the new entry.

If you want to change one of the preset sizes, click on the corresponding entry, for example, for the width or the height.

3 Assign the new values for the height and width.

If you only assign one value (either for the width or the height), the window adjusts only that one, and keeps the previous value for the other.

4 Click on the DESCRIPTION field and enter a short text.

5 With *OK* or, alternatively, by double clicking the ⏎ key, you save the settings and return to the document window.

CAUTION

The given window size is displaying the content window of the browsers, without a menu bar or frames. After this, the actual screen size is displayed in brackets. For example, 955x600 pixels corresponds to a screen size of 1024x768 pixels.

To the right of the pop-up window, you can see the estimated **file size** and loading time for the Web page.

In addition to the actual HTML document, all of the integrated files, such as images and other media elements, are considered in this download time. These statistics are based on a 28.8 KB/sec modem. This default setup in Dreamweaver can be found in the STATUS BAR menu and can be modified in PREFERENCES (see above).

The **Mini-Launcher** is in the right corner of the status bar.

Here, there are similar buttons to those in the launcher, which we will describe below. Here you will read which functions you can call.

In EDIT/PREFERENCES/STATUS BAR, you can insert and remove this launcher bar. To do this, tick the SHOW LAUNCHER IN STATUS BAR check box.

Rulers

To make sure that you can develop a page more quickly and more precisely, Dreamweaver has several aids available.

The ruler at the top and left edge of the document window is an extremely important tool.

Unit of Measurement: Pixel

Zero point

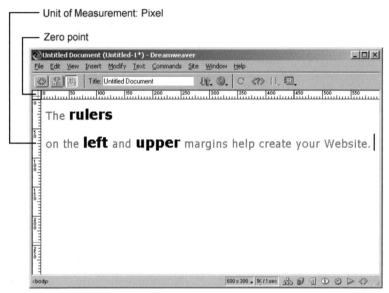

To turn the ruler on or off, select VIEW/RULERS/SHOW or press the [Ctrl] + [Alt] + [⇧] + [R] keys. If the ruler is shown, a tick will appear next to the menu entry.

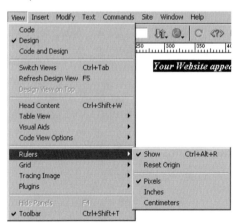

How to change the ruler entities:

- From the VIEW/RULERS menu bar, select the preferred measurement: pixels, inches or centimetres. The measurement you decide to use will likewise be ticked.

In Dreamweaver, you can change the **position of the zero point**:

1 Click on the zero point in the upper left corner of the document window.

2 Keep the left mouse button pressed and move the zero point to the preferred position. A cross-line will appear.

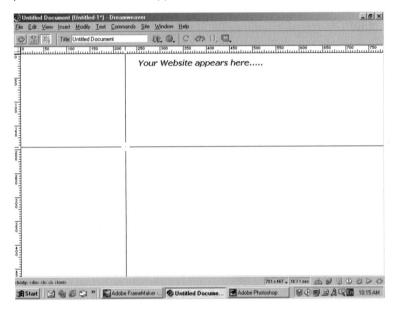

3 In VIEW/RULER/RESET ORIGINAL, reset the zero point to the starting position.

Grids

A grid is another option to help you lay out your page.

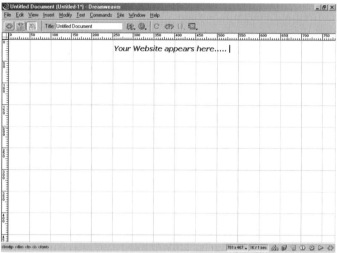

To display the grid, select VIEW/GRID/SHOW ([Ctrl] + [Alt] + [G]) from the menu bar in the document window.

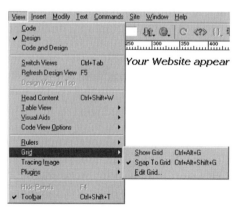

You can bring the layers (see Chapter 9) into line with the grid, and therefore position them exactly (VIEW/GRID/SNAP TO GRID, or, alternatively, [Ctrl] + [Alt] + [⇧] + [G]).

Select VIEW/GRID/EDIT GRID to work with further grid options. In the GRID SETTINGS dialog box, you can colour, define the spacing and display the grid as lines or dots.

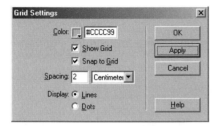

Invisible elements

As already mentioned, the display in the Dreamweaver window is very close to the actual representation in the Web browser. However, the invisible elements are an exception. These are only visible in Dreamweaver and not in the Web browser.

There are a few examples to be seen in the following figure:

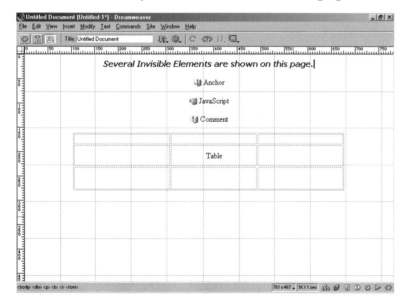

How invisible elements are displayed:

1 Select EDIT/PREFERENCES/INVISIBLE ELEMENTS, to be found in the menu bar of the document window.

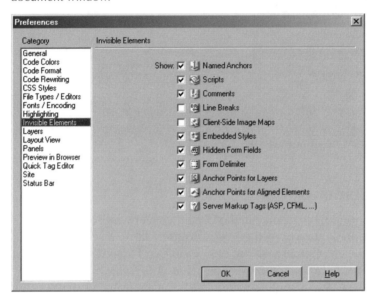

2 Every selected invisible element has an activated check box. Here, you can also remove elements from the view.

3 Confirm your selections with OK. The selected invisible elements are now displayed as icons in the document window.

> **NOTE**
>
> *All the invisible elements will be explained in the corresponding chapter. In the PREFERENCES/INVISIBLE ELEMENTS dialog box, you can see an overview of all the icons used.*
>
> *You can examine the selected invisible elements in the Property Inspector (see The Property Inspector on page 31).*

The icon bar

The upper toolbar under the menu bar is available for the first time in the new Dreamweaver 4.

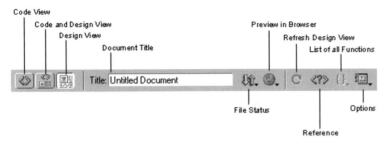

On this, you will find buttons and pop-up menus with which you can navigate through the entire document window. You can also switch between individual views more quickly and directly using this tool bar. On this bar, there are several options available, such as, for example, previewing in the browser.

Using the first three buttons, you decide what you want to display in the document window. It is also possible to call this view from the menu bar in VIEW. In the new Dreamweaver version, you can place the HTML Source Inspector directly in the document window.

Button	Menu bar	Description/Effect
	VIEW/CODE	displays the HTML source code ()
	VIEW/CODE AND DESIGN	opens the source code and layout window ()
	VIEW/DESIGN	the layout window becomes active

Table 1.2: Description of the different buttons in the symbol menu

Every modification to the HTML Source Inspector will be shown in the document window. At the same time, every modification to the document window will be reflected in the HTML code in the HTML Source Inspector.

In the sections about the HTML editor and the HTML Source Inspector, I will discuss the options of editing the source code further.

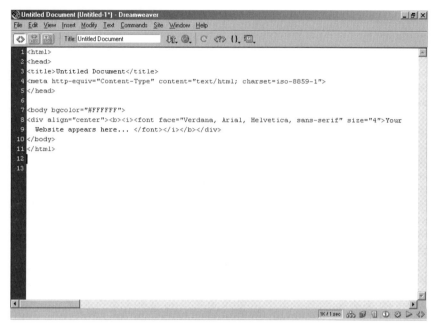

Figure 1.2: The HTML view in the document window

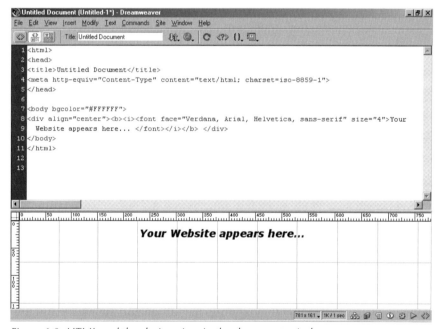

Figure 1.3: HTML and the design view in the document window

With VIEW/DESIGN VIEW ON TOP the setup of the individual areas is changed.

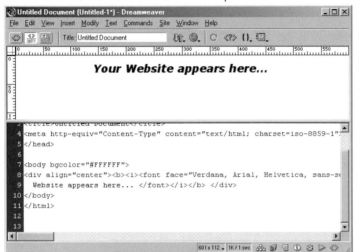

I have turned off the tool bar in order to have more space available. To do this, you select VIEW/TOOL BAR in the menu bar. The corresponding keyboard shortcut is: Ctrl + ⇧ + T.

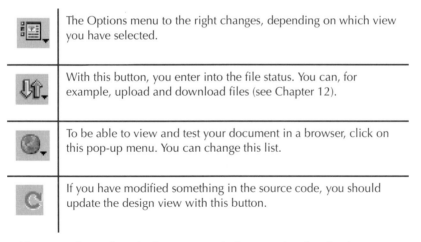

	The Options menu to the right changes, depending on which view you have selected.
	With this button, you enter into the file status. You can, for example, upload and download files (see Chapter 12).
	To be able to view and test your document in a browser, click on this pop-up menu. You can change this list.
	If you have modified something in the source code, you should update the design view with this button.

Table 1.3: The toolbar also has commands that are related to the document status

27

How to add browsers in the PREVIEW IN BROWSER:

1 Click on the PREVIEW IN BROWSER 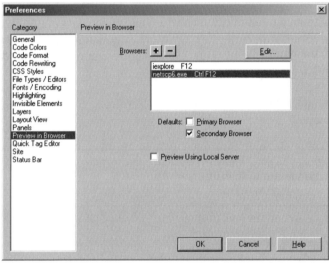 button in the toolbar. Select EDIT BROWSER LIST.

2 Or, go to the menu bar and select EDIT/PREFERENCES/PREVIEW IN BROWSER.

3 Click on the (+) button and select the program on your computer.

How to remove a browser from the list:

1 Highlight it.

2 Press the ⊟ key.

3 Confirm with OK.

Selecting objects

There are several options for selecting objects on a Web page.

- Double click on the selected **word**. Now it is highlighted.

- To highlight a **text area**, left click on it in the design window or press ⬆
  + ⬅ or ➡.

- You highlight an **HTML row** by clicking on the corresponding row
  number on the left edge of your HTML editor. These must therefore be
  visible. If you would like to be shown the row number, click on the VIEW
  OPTIONS 🔲 button in the tool bar and then select the **row numbers**
  command.

- Click once on an **image**. This is how you select it.

- The quickest way to select a **table** is to right click on it and simultaneously
  press Ctrl.

- You can use the menu bar: select MODIFY/TABLE/SELECT TABLE. Another
  option is to place the cursor in the table and then select it with the Ctrl +
  A keyboard shortcuts.

> **TIP**
>
> *In Dreamweaver 4, you are able to highlight several cells in a table at
> the same time. They do not need to be next to each other.*
>
> *Click on the cell while pressing the Ctrl key. Continue the action for as
> long as it is necessary to select what you wish to select.*

Highlighted objects can be cut out, copied, moved and erased. In addition,
you can change their properties.

Either way, if you work in the design or the code view, the marked area will
simultaneously be highlighted in the other window area. An object marked
in the design window is, at the same time, also marked in the HTML source
code. On the other hand, the parallel source code is also selected in the
design view.

29

In this way, you can quickly identify specific elements in the HTML source code.

Anyone who is already familiar with the source code can select code and design elements with the **Tag Selector**.

In the following example, the highlighted table cell will be marked with the Tag Selector. The corresponding HTML source code will also be highlighted simultaneously.

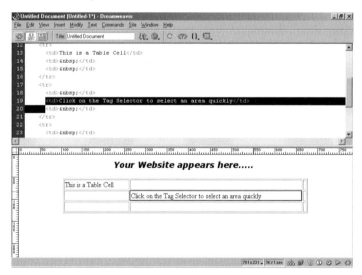

If you would like to mark a paragraph, click on a word in the paragraph. Then press **<p>** in the Tag Selector. **<p>** stands for paragraph.

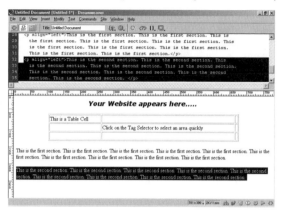

The Tag-in-Tag Selector simplifies the selection of tables, links and the **<body>** of a page. However, in order to be able to work with it, it is necessary to have some knowledge of HTML.

The Property Inspector

You can modify the features of the selected text or objects in the Property Inspector. The Property Inspector changes its appearance according to which object is selected.

The Property Inspector can, for example, look like this when a text area has been highlighted.

31

When a table is highlighted, it looks somewhat different:

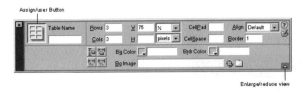

To confirm a modified property, you could either click top left on the APPLY button or press ⏎. If you leave the Inspector, the settings will, as a rule, be automatically taken on.

> **NOTE**
>
> *When text is selected, there will be no APPLY button available. For all of the other elements such as images, tables, Flash movies, forms or layers, a graphic of the element will appear in the APPLY button. It carries the names of the objects.*

Using the expander arrow on the right, you can enlarge or reduce the Inspector.

You open and close the Property Inspector in WINDOW/PROPERTIES or with Ctrl + F3.

> **TIP**
>
> *Context menus offer quick access to essential settings for the current selection. Right click on the object. Select the desired commands from the context menu that opens.*

The Launcher

To turn the Launcher on or off, select WINDOW/LAUNCHER. The Launcher is a floating panel with which you can call further windows.

The launcher buttons open the Site window, the Library panel, the HTML Styles panel, the CSS Style panel, the Behaviours Inspector, the History panel and the HTML Source Inspector by default.

The icons appear below the document window, as well as in the Mini-Launcher bar.

NOTE

Click on the orientation icon in the right lower corner of the Launcher. Using this, you can switch the orientation from vertical to horizontal.

TIP

Activate the SHOW LAUNCHER IN STATUS BAR check box, under EDIT/ PREFERENCES/STATUS BAR. By doing so, you save space and keep an overview more easily.

To set up the Launcher bar:

1 Select EDIT/PREFERENCES and click on PANELS in the list.

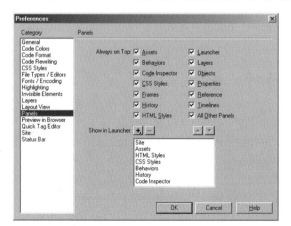

2 You can see which buttons appear in the Launcher, under SHOW IN LAUNCHER.

3 Click on the plus button (+) to add another button.

4 If you want to delete a button, highlight it and click on the minus button (–).

5 To change the order of the icons in the Launcher bar, mark the corresponding item and click the left arrow box until you reach the position you desire. If you move an item further down the list, you are moving the icon to the right in the Launcher bar.

6 Confirm your changes with OK.

7 Now your changes are activated.

The Object palette

Open the Object palette using the menu bar WINDOW/OBJECTS.

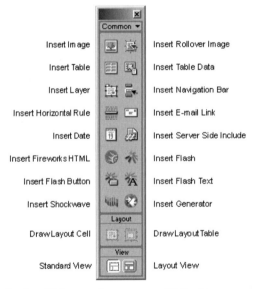

Insert Image		Insert Rollover Image
Insert Table		Insert Table Data
Insert Layer		Insert Navigation Bar
Insert Horizontal Rule		Insert E-mail Link
Insert Date		Insert Server Side Include
Insert Fireworks HTML		Insert Flash
Insert Flash Button		Insert Flash Text
Insert Shockwave		Insert Generator
Draw Layout Cell		Draw Layout Table
Standard View		Layout View

In the Object palette, you will find buttons with which you can integrate and develop various object types. Images, tables, layers and frames belong to this Object palette.

By using the Object palette, you are also able to switch between the Standard and Layout views. As well as this, the layout character elements are also available. Further information about these will be found in Chapter 6.

As well as the common menu, there are several menus for specific elements, where specialised menus are integrated: Forms, Frames, Head, Special, Invisible elements and Characters. To call these, just click on the drop-down menu in the upper right corner of the object manager.

We will be working with the Object palette in later chapters. You will then learn, step by step, how the objects are inserted.

How to change the setup of the Object palette:

1 Select EDIT/PREFERENCES and go to GENERAL.

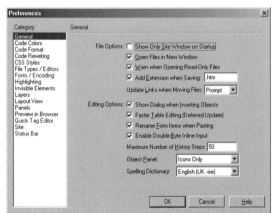

2 Under OBJECT PANEL, specify whether you only want icons, just text or both to be displayed.

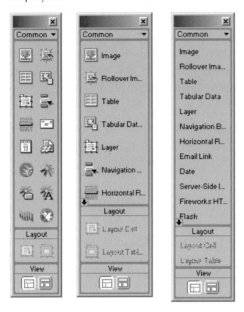

3 You can also specify whether, every time you insert an object, a dialog box should appear, and you can also, for example, ask for the directory in which the file is placed.

The History window

Select WINDOW/HISTORY or press ⬆ + F10.

The History window lists all of the steps you have taken so far in the active window.

You can undo one or several stages with the History panel. In addition to this, you can develop commands which automate recurrent tasks.

How to undo one or several steps:

1 The pointer on the left edge displays the latest actions. Drag the pointer from the left window edge to the desired position.

2 The undone actions are now shown in grey.

If you have undone some actions, the deleted steps will no longer be displayed in the History panel.

Since you now know and are familiar with the basics of Dreamweaver and how the program is built up, we can start with some practical work.

Chapter 2

The first Web site

In this workshop, you will learn how to construct, open, save and print a Web page. We will determine the page properties and general properties for the objects. Following this, you will learn how to create the basic infrastructure for sound site management.

When creating a document in Dreamweaver, you have several options. You can set up an empty page, open an existing HTML document, or develop a new document on the basis of a template.

When you start up the program, Dreamweaver automatically sets up an empty document page.

WHAT IS THIS?

Templates *are pre-designed patterns determining the layout of a page. In Dreamweaver, you are able to construct this master page yourself.*

*A **Web site** consists of several linked HTML documents. They have a similar design, they usually deal with similar or related subjects and they serve the same purpose.*

Creating a new HTML page

To create a new, empty HTML page in Dreamweaver, proceed as follows:

1 Select FILE/NEW ([Ctrl] + [N]) in the document window.

2 Or go to the site window and click on FILE/NEW WINDOW.

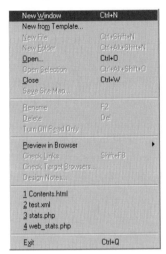

3 A new document window is opened.

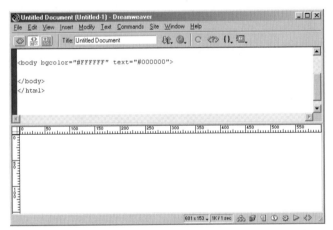

You will notice in the HTML Source Inspector that the document is not completely empty. It already contains the following tags: **<html>**, **<head>** and **<body>** and the end tags of these.

If you now insert text, images, tables and other elements into the document (we will see later how this is done), you can see how the source code will be constructed simultaneously.

Opening an existing HTML page

If, by now, you have created an HTML file, you could open and edit this in Dreamweaver. It is not necessary to have originally created the file in Dreamweaver.

In addition, you can open text files, such as, for example, JavaScript, in Dreamweaver.

1 Select FILE/OPEN from the menu bar in the document window.

2 The OPEN FILE dialog box appears. By default, Dreamweaver always shows the directory which was opened last.

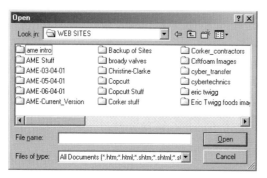

3 If you only want to be shown a particular file type, you decide this in the lower dialog box.

4 Should the file be in another directory, search through the directories on your computer until you have found the desired file.

5 Click on the file. The file name is now displayed in the FILE NAME list box.

6 Click on the OPEN button or confirm with ⏎.

7 The file is opened in the document window.

TIP

The four last opened HTML documents are shown under FILE in the menu bar. Click on one and the document will be opened directly.

New	Ctrl+N
New from Template...	
Open...	Ctrl+O
Open in Frame...	Ctrl+Shift+O
Close	Ctrl+W
Save	Ctrl+S
Save As...	Ctrl+Shift+S
Save as Template...	
Save All Frames	
Revert	
Import	▶
Export	▶
Convert	▶
Preview in Browser	▶
Debug in Browser	▶
Check Links	Shift+F8
Check Target Browsers...	
Design Notes...	
1 index.htm	
2 index2.htm	
3 Contents.html	
4 test.xml	
Exit	Ctrl+Q

NOTE

A document created in Microsoft Word will be opened using the FILE/IMPORT/IMPORT WORD HTML menu (see Chapter 3).

Saving

Make sure you save your work regularly. It is always very annoying if the computer suddenly crashes or something else goes wrong. Play it safe.

1 Select FILE/SAVE AS. The SAVE AS dialog box appears.

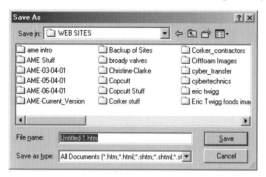

2 Go to the directory where you want to save your file.

3 Name the file.

4 If you would like to use other file extensions (such as `.cgi` or `.asp`), you will need to determine the file type.

> **NOTE**
>
> *PCs adds the* `.htm` *extension to HTML files by default. Macs, on the other hand, use the* `.html` *extension. You will not need to add the file extension yourself.*

5 Click on the SAVE button, or confirm your input with ⏎.

> **CAUTION**
>
> ***Conventions for assigning file names***
>
> *When you save your document, you should avoid blank spaces and special characters in the file and directory name. Many servers will alter these characters during file uploads. All the references to the file are then broken.*

If you want to close a file that has not been saved, the following dialog box will appear:

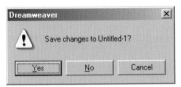

Click on YES and the dialog window SAVE AS appears. If you click on NO, the file will be closed without being saved. Click on CANCEL and the HTML document remains open.

Page properties

In contrast to elements, which only relate to certain objects, page properties apply to the whole page.

The page name, the background image, the background colour, the colour of the text and hyperlinks, as well as page borders, are all visual page properties. Other properties concern the coding of the document and the tracing image.

- Open the PAGE PROPERTIES dialog box under MODIFY/PAGE PROPERTIES or press Ctrl + J. The PAGE PROPERTIES dialog box will be opened.

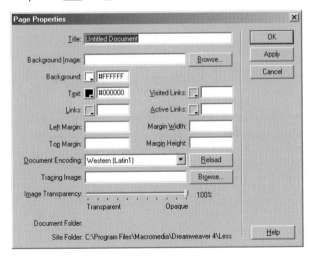

The page title

1 Open the PAGE PROPERTIES dialog box as described above.

2 By default, the title is "Untitled document". Replace this temporary name.

3 Click on OK to close the dialog box or go ahead and change more of the page properties.

4 The page title appears in the Dreamweaver title bar. The page title is shown in the browser title bar as well.

NOTE

*The page name is saved in the **<head>** tag.*

TIP

You don't need to assign a page name. In fact, all pages are named with "untitled document". But you really should change this name, because search engines (see Appendix) use it in the index. That is why you should select a meaningful name for the page title.

WHAT IS THIS?

*Every HTML document has a **<body>** as well as a **<head>**. The **<head>** is the top part of an HTML file. It contains statements and instructions for Web browsers, servers and search engines.*

The background

In the PAGE PROPERTIES dialog box, you determine the background image and the background colour of a page. If you define both at the same time, the background colour will be displayed first, while the background image is loading. Afterwards, the image will overlap the background colour. If the image has transparent pixels, the background colour will shine through.

How to define background image or background colour:

1 Select MODIFY/PAGE PROPERTIES or right click in the design view to open the corresponding context menu. Likewise, click here on the page properties.

2 To select a background image, click on the BROWSE button. The SELECT IMAGE SOURCE dialog box appears.

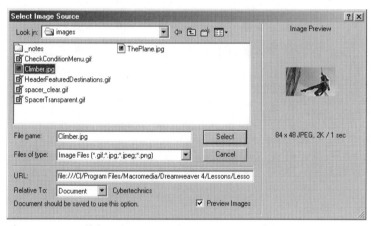

The image will be shown in the preview. After that, the image size and the download time will be calculated.

You can, of course, insert the path and the file name directly in the input field, if you know them.

A background image will be tiled if it doesn't cover the whole design window. Dreamweaver shows the tiling effect as it will look in the browser.

A tiled background image will be repeated both from left to right and from top to bottom, until the window is covered.

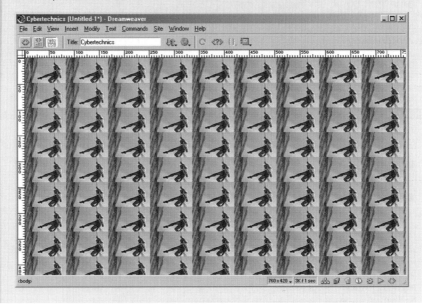

3 You set the background colour by clicking on the corresponding colour box. Select a colour with the eyedropper from the now opened colour panel.

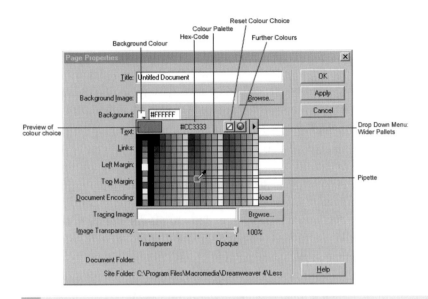

TIP

You can also select colours from outside the Dreamweaver colour panel with the eyedropper. In this way, you can leave the Dreamweaver window and pick up colours from other applications. If you would like to return to Dreamweaver, click on any of the Dreamweaver windows and continue your work.

4 To bring up more panels, click on the drop-down menu on the top right.

Dreamweaver shows the **colour cubes** by default. When selecting, make sure that only COLOR CUBES and CONTINUOUS TONE are Web safe.

You delete the current colour either by selecting a new colour or by clicking
on the crossed button (DEFAULT COLOR).

If you click on the SYSTEM COLOR PICKER ⬤ you could choose from millions
of colours in the dialog box that appears.

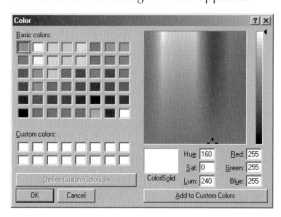

Text and links

By default, the text colour on a Web page is black. You should change the
text colour for pages with dark background colour. Make sure that the text is
readable. Create a harmonic colour scheme for your Web page.

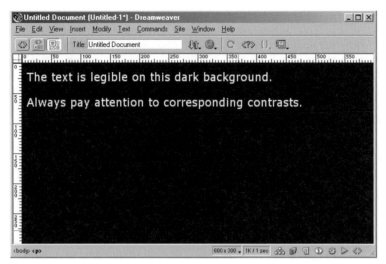

In the PAGE PROPERTIES dialog box (see above), you could apply corresponding colours to hyperlinks, visited and active links as well as text. Proceed in the way described in the section regarding the background.

NOTE

The active link colour appears while you are clicking on the link.

You can modify the set text colour used for the **<body>**. You can determine the colour for the corresponding text area (see Chapter 3).

Page margins

Left margin and **top margin** mostly determine the page margins. However, these **<body>** inputs can only be interpreted in Internet Explorer. Netscape ignores these values and interprets them as **margin width** and **margin height** instead. Again, these cannot be interpreted in Internet Explorer.

You should use all four inputs in order to get the best presentation in all kinds of browsers.

CAUTION

Dreamweaver does not display the page margins in the document window. Therefore, you should preview in a browser (see the section Previews in the browser on page 53).

Document encoding

With this drop-down menu, you state how the browser should interpret the specific characters of your document. Select Western if you are dealing with English or other West European languages.

There are additional options available for Central European languages, Cyrillic, Greek, Icelandic, Japanese, Chinese and Korean.

> **TIP**
>
> *To change the character set, go to EDIT/PREFERENCES/FONTS/ ENCODING. This setting has no influence on how the visitor sees the text on your page.*

Tracing images

In Dreamweaver, you could place a graphic in the background and use this as a pattern for the construction of the actual page. This tracing image is merely a design aid. The image will not be saved in the source code, and will therefore not be shown in a browser.

How to place a tracing image in your document window:

1 Click in the PAGE PROPERTIES dialog box on the corresponding BROWSE button.

2 Select the desired image in the dialog box. The graphic must be available as a JPEG, GIF or PNG. You can also get to this window via VIEW/TRACING IMAGE/LOAD.

3 In Page Properties, set the transparency of the tracing image with the image transparency slider.

> **NOTE**
>
> *If you use a tracing image, the actual background image in the source code will no longer be visible in Dreamweaver. However, nothing is changed in the browser view.*

How to hide or show the tracing image:

- Select VIEW/TRACING IMAGE/SHOW in the menu bar. If there is a tick behind this command, the tracing image is shown.

How to change the position of the tracing image:

1 Click on VIEW/TRACING IMAGE/ADJUST POSITION in the menu bar.

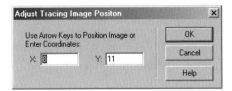

2 Give values for the X and Y positions, or move the image to the desired position with the arrow key.

> **TIP**
>
> *To move an image 5 pixels at a time, press on* ⇧ *simultaneously with the key arrow.*

How to reset the position of the tracing image to zero on the X/Y axis:

- Select VIEW/TRACING IMAGE/RESET POSITION. The tracing image returns to the original position in the upper left corner.

How to assign the tracing image to a chosen element:

1 Select an element in the document window.

2 Go to VIEW/TRACING IMAGE /ALIGN WITH SELECTION.

The upper left corner of the **tracing image** is now adjusted on the upper left corner of the selected element.

Previews in the browser

You can check your work at any time in a Web browser.

1 Select FILE/PREVIEW IN BROWSER. Go to the displayed browser name. Internet Explorer is used in our example. Or just press F12.

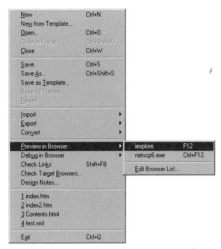

- If your browser is not open, Dreamweaver will start it automatically and load the relevant page.

- If your browser is already open, Dreamweaver loads the page in a new browser window.

2 Return to Dreamweaver using the task bar and edit your document.

NOTE

Dreamweaver creates a temporary file for displaying in the browser. Changes will only be shown by using F12. *The buttons REFRESH or RELOAD in your browser do not show the current version of your work.*

You can always save the Dreamweaver document every time and view it in the browser by going to FILE/OPEN. In this case, you will be able to see the intended effect on the updated page.

Go to FILE/PREVIEW IN BROWSER/EDIT BROWSER LIST to add new browsers with (+) or to delete with (–) existing ones in the browser preview.

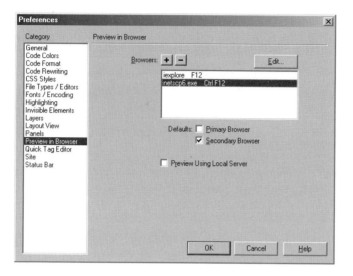

Printing

Dreamweaver is not equipped with a printing function. If you would like to print your page, either go to preview in the browser or open the saved file. Then select FILE/PRINT or click on the print button.

Local site and project management

A local site is a gathering of several pages, saved either on your computer or in a local network, that later will be launched on the Internet. It is not absolutely necessary that they are placed in the same directory. The file manager in Dreamweaver helps you to find the required images, Web pages and the integrated elements (see Chapter 4).

Dreamweaver makes it easier for you to manage your links. If you change a file name, or move the file to another directory, Dreamweaver will automatically update all the links to this page.

The site window is a powerful tool for planning and management of pages, as well as being completely able to function as an FTP Client (see Chapter 12).

Open the site window in which you go to the menu bar WINDOW/SITE FILES, or press F8.

The site window appears. When you open it for the first time, you will not see a single file. That is why you must create it.

> **TIP**
>
> *All column headlines are buttons as well. When you click on them, the files are organised accordingly.*
>
> *You can change the column width here.*

Constructing, editing and deleting the local site

To construct a local site, you need a site root. It does not matter whether the site contains an existing Web page, or whether a new one is to be created.

How to determine a local site root:

1 Select SITE/DEFINE SITES in the menu bar of the document window or the site window. The DEFINE SITES dialog window appears.

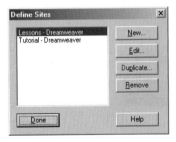

2 Click on NEW to open the SITE DEFINITION dialog box.

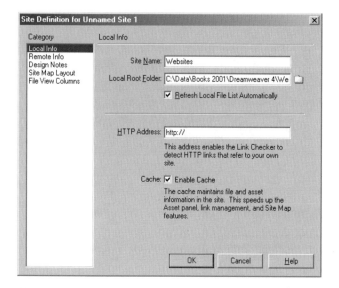

3 Enter the site name.

4 Name the local directory or click on the button next to it and navigate to the corresponding directory.

5 Select the directory you want as site root for your local site client.

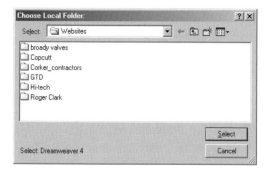

6 Go to the displayed OPEN button, and then to SELECT. The path will be displayed in the previous dialog box.

7 Make sure that **Local Info** is highlighted in the category list.

8 Click on OK to close the dialog window.

9 In the DEFINE SITES dialog window, confirm your setup with DONE.

If you activate the cache check box in the SITE DEFINITION dialog window, the following confirmation appears:

Click on OK. Dreamweaver then sets up the cache. The action will only take a few seconds.

In addition to this, you can edit or delete a local site in the DEFINE SITES dialog window:

- If you would like to edit your local site, click on the EDIT button. The SITE DEFINITION dialog window appears (see above). Make the necessary changes.

- To delete a local site, click on REMOVE. A dialog box appears, which, for safety reasons, asks if you really want to delete the site.

Dreamweaver removes the site from the overview in the DEFINE SITES window. Files are not deleted with this. Only the site entry has been removed from the list in the DEFINE SITES dialog window.

The most important file management functions in the site window:

1 Open page: If you double click on the HTML files in the site window, the file will be opened in a document window.

2 Create new files: Go to the location where the new file should be created. Select FILE/NEW WINDOW. A new file appears. Name the file.

3 Create new folder: Go to the location where the new folder should be created. Select FILE/NEW. A new folder appears. Name the folder.

4 Preview in browser: Right click on the HTML file. The context menu appears. Select PREVIEW IN BROWSER and the browser (cf. the Previews in the browser section). Or select FILE/PREVIEW IN BROWSER in the menu bar of the site window.

5 Remove files or folders: Right click on the file or the folder. Select DELETE in the context menu. A dialog box appears. Confirm with OK.

6 Rename file or folder: Right click once on the file or folder you want to rename. The name now appears framed.

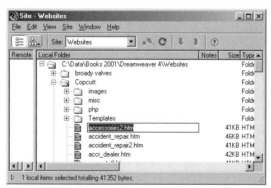

Now type in the new name and confirm it with [↵]. The UPDATE dialog box appears.

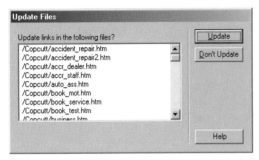

Click on UPDATE to automatically update all the links that refer to this file or folder. For this purpose you must have created the cache in the SITE DEFINITION dialog window.

If you have not determined a cache, this dialog box appears:

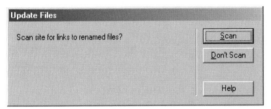

Decide whether you want to scan for links to the renamed or moved file or folder.

7 **Move file or folder:** Click on the file or folder that you want to move. Drag this to the new position while pressing the mouse button. If you would like to move several files/folders at the same time, you can do this by holding down the ⬆ or Ctrl key.

Defining the homepage

1 Highlight the HTML file, which should be defined as homepage.

2 Select SET AS HOMEPAGE in the opened context menu.

Now you can graphically view the links coming from the homepage in the site map. Therefore, select the  button in the site window. Then select the desired view in the sub menu:

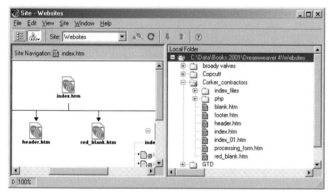

NOTE

To display the site map, you will need to define a homepage for your site. This is also the start page of your map.

Symbols in the site map

In the site map, the HTML files and other page elements are represented as icons.

Table 2.1 gives a brief overview.

	Broken link.
	Directs to a file in another site or a special link (e.g. e-mail or script reference).
	You have checked this file.
	Somebody else has checked this file.
	Read-only file.

Table 2.1: Icons used in the site map

Managing Web sites

Before you publish your pages online (see Chapter 12), you should have tested them sufficiently on your own system. Carry out changes offline. Check content, navigation and the Web design thoroughly before you publish these. This procedure will save you an awful lot of stress and trouble.

TIP

Create the site structure with a sensible administration of the individual documents in various directories.

- *Create a separate folder for the project.*

- *Store topic-related pages in the same directory.*

- *Consider where it is best to place files, images, Flash files and other elements. I always place images in a separate image folder within a category. This has the advantage that all the graphics appearing in this topic will be saved centrally and are therefore quick to find.*

Chapter 3

Text and paragraphs

In this chapter, you will learn how to format text. You will learn how to define font, font size and the colour of the font, and how to insert special characters. I will then show you how to structure the text into paragraphs and thus determine the layout of the page.

By now, you know the basic options and functions in Dreamweaver 4. You have surely also laid your foundations for your Web site. In this, and the following chapters, you will learn about what kind of content you can add to your page. The following chapters will also deal with further content elements, such as images, animation, scripts, etc.

You will find it simple to format text and sections in Dreamweaver. The formatting functions are very similar to those of a normal word processing program. There is no need for you to have prior knowledge of HTML, but feel free to use this if you have it.

Placing text

You can either use texts from other HTML documents and other files (such as Word or Excel) or type directly into the HTML document.

How to insert text from another document or from another file:

1 Mark the text you want to copy.

2 Press Ctrl + C. The text is now in the clipboard.

3 Go to the design view window of your Dreamweaver document.

4 Press Ctrl + V or select EDIT/PASTE from the menu bar. The text will now be inserted into the document.

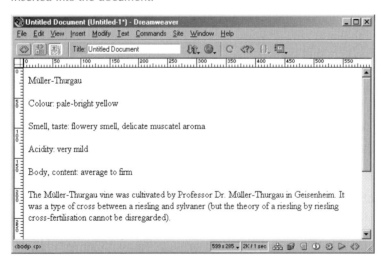

Or:

1 Save the document as an HTML file in the other application (such as Excel).

2 Open the HTML file in Dreamweaver.

> **CAUTION**
>
> *When you copy text to the clipboard, formatting will not be adopted by Dreamweaver when the copy is inserted. The paragraphs are also lost. Line breaks remain unchanged.*

A file created in Microsoft Word can be opened in the menu FILE/IMPORT/ IMPORT WORD HTML. Dreamweaver opens the file and at the same time removes the unnecessary HTML code generated by Microsoft Word when saved in the HTML format.

> **CAUTION**
>
> *You cannot open a Word file (.doc) directly in Dreamweaver. If you want to import the content of a Word file, you will first have to save it as an HTML file. You open this as described above.*

Formatting text

If you have already worked with Word, you will know the basics of text formatting. Formatting text in Dreamweaver is just as simple.

As soon as the text is opened in Dreamweaver, you can work on it in the same way as you are used to in a word processing program.

Open the Property Inspector from WINDOW/PROPERTIES or press Ctrl + F3.

As described in the first chapter, this changes its appearance depending on what you highlight in the document window.

You can modify existing text formats and create new ones. Furthermore, you can align sections (see Aligning paragraphs on page 93), create lists (see page 89) and create hyperlinks (see Chapter 5) to determine specific text paths.

To see the text properties, click on the words or in the paragraph. You can also mark the corresponding text.

TIP

Click on the arrow on the bottom right to display further options or to remove them again.

Defining font

You should always assign a font to your documents. If you don't do this, text will be displayed in the font installed on the reader's Web browser, which does not always suit the overall image of a Web page.

To assign a specific typography style to letters, words or whole paragraphs, proceed as follows:

1 Mark the text you want to format.

2 Open the Property Inspector.

3 Select the font combination you prefer in the Property Inspector. The drop-down menu has three fonts in each combination.

> **NOTE**
>
> *The most frequent font combination used is already established in Dreamweaver.*

4 Or enter the preferred font directly in the menu (where you must type over the **default font**).

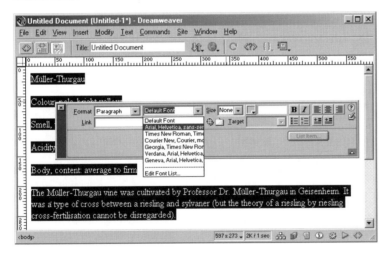

> **TIP**
>
> *Always name two or three fonts. If the first choice is not installed on the user's system (the user of your page), the second choice will be displayed. Everybody can define these individually in the browser preferences.*

You can also define a font from the menu in the document window:

1 Mark the text you want to format.

2 Go to TEXT/FONT in the menu bar of the document window.

3 Select a font combination from the sub menu now opened.

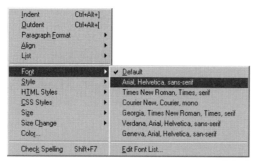

The displayed font combination in the Property Inspector and the menu bar can be changed, enlarged and deleted as you like:

1 Select TEXT/FONT/EDIT FONT LIST. The EDIT FONT LIST dialog box appears.

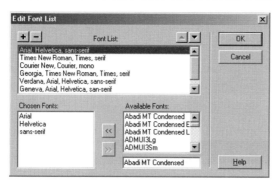

2 In the dialog box, mark the desired font combination. This will now be transferred to the lower left field.

Delete a font combination:

1 In the upper list, mark the font combination you would like to remove.

2 Click on (—). The font combination is now removed.

3 Confirm your changes with the OK button.

CAUTION

Dreamweaver will not ask whether you really want to delete the font combination.

Adding font combinations:

1 Click on the (+) button in the upper left corner of the window.

2 From the left list, select the fonts you would like to have in a combination. This list contains all the fonts installed on your computer.

3 Click on the << button if you would like to add a font. Click on >> if you would like to remove a font from the combination.

4 To add further fonts, repeat steps 2 and 3. You should not define more than three fonts per combination. You should, in addition, select a third generic font family.

5 The selected fonts appear in the CHOSEN FONTS box.

6 Confirm with OK. The font combination now appears in the menu bar and in the Property Inspector.

NOTE

*If none of the given fonts is installed on the user's computer, the text will be displayed in the default font of the respective **generic font family**.*

These generic fonts include: Cursive, Fantasy, Monospace, Sans Serif and Serif.

Example: the default font for Monospace on most computers is Courier.

How to remove a font from a combination:

1 Click on the (+) button in the upper left corner of the window.

2 Select the font from the list below that you would like to remove from the combination.

3 Click on the **>>** button. By doing so, you have removed the font from the combination.

4 Confirm with OK.

> **NOTE**
>
> *If you would like to add a font that is not installed on your computer, go to the AVAILABLE FONTS text box with the font names and click on the << button.*

Font style

To change the **font style**, click on **Bold** **B** or **I** *Italic* in the Property Inspector. These are the only two options in the Property Inspector. B stands for **bold**; I stands for **italic**.

Alternatively, select TEXT/STYLE in the sub menu. Here, you have more possibilities (e.g. **Bold**, *Italic*, <u>Underline</u>).

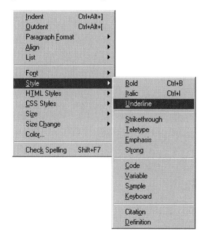

NOTE

*There are **physical and logical styles** which determine the appearance of the text: with physical styles you determine the appearance of a text quite precisely. For example, with the <b> tag, you specify that the surrounded text is to be displayed in bold.*

On the other hand, the logical style only determines the character of a text approximately and leaves the exact interpretation to the browser. In the same way, <strong> merely defines that the surrounded text is to be highlighted. Most graphical browsers will then show this text in bold letters, but there may well be some that will interpret it differently.

Font size

In the Property Inspector, or in the TEXT/SIZE sub menu, select the desired absolute size (1 to 7).

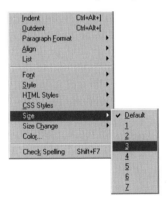

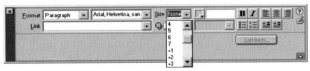

In Dreamweaver, you can also specify font sizes (+1 to +7 and –1 to –7). For this, you can use the Property Inspector as usual. If you would like to define this using the menu bar, the entry is available from TEXT/SIZE CHANGE.

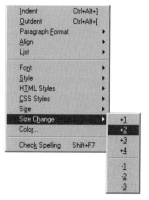

The positive and negative numbers are based on the basefont size. If a <basefont> font size is missing, a default of 3 is interpreted. Select the relative font size +3, being the value 6 if you then enter -1, the displayed font size will be 2. The font size is always between 1 and 7. Minimum and maximum font sizes are not exceeded in any of the examples:

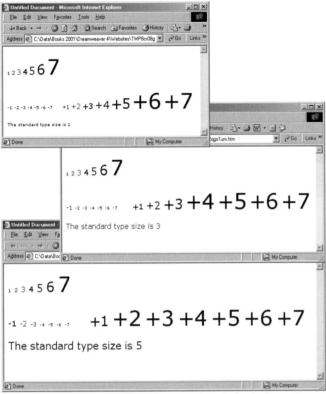

Of course, you can also change the default font size of a document in the `<basefont>` tag:

1 Open the HTML Source Inspector.

2 Type in the following line of code directly after the `<body>` tag: `<basefont size=n>`. Replace n with a value from 1 to 7. There is no end tag.

3 You will see no changes in Dreamweaver. To check this, go to the PREVIEW IN BROWSER button, or press F12.

Text colour

In the Page Properties (see Chapter 2), you have set a general colour for the text. However, you can change this for single words or text blocks.

How to change the colour of a text:

1 Mark the text area.

2 Select the desired colour from the colour box in the Property Inspector.

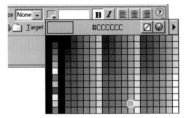

You can access the shown Web safe palette, use other palettes or mix a colour yourself (see Chapter 2). The hexadecimal code will be generated automatically. A larger colour preview is found to the left above the palette. Beside it is the hex code.

3 As soon as you select a colour, the palette will be closed. The previously highlighted text area is now coloured.

• Alternatively, indicate the name or the hexadecimal code of the colour directly in the box next to the colour box. Don't forget the rhombus.

• Or, select TEXT/COLOR from the menu bar. The COLOR window appears.

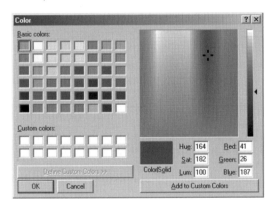

An example of a formatted text:

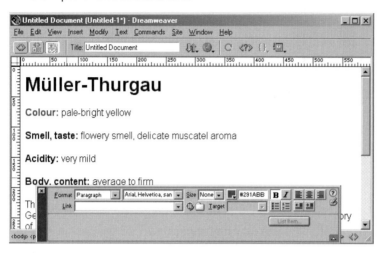

In this document, the heading is determined with <h1>. The text colour was changed. In addition, words were highlighted in **bold**.

Special characters

HTML tags consist of ASCII characters and are taken from English language concepts. The characters on your keyboard correspond largely to this ASCII typesetting.

Nevertheless, this character set is not always sufficient, and therefore there are a number of special characters. You can also use special characters in HTML.

1 Open the object panel using the WINDOW/OBJECTS menu bar or alternatively select Ctrl + F2.

2 By default, the common object panel will be displayed first. Click on CHARACTERS to bring the special characters panel to the fore.

3 Mark the area where you want to insert the characters.

4 Click on the characters that you want to insert. The special characters will be placed in the corresponding place.

> **NOTE**
>
> *If you have a look at the HTML code of a special character, you will almost always state a similar structure. For example, the source code for the copyright symbol is ©. Also, many other characters start with the ampersand. Behind this comes the name of the sign, followed by the final semicolon. You will find an overview of the most important special characters in the Appendix.*

If you want to use a special character not found in this panel, select INSERT/ SPECIAL CHARACTERS from the menu bar.

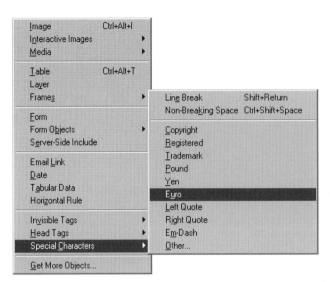

Select INSERT/SPECIAL CHARACTERS/OTHER... to choose further characters.

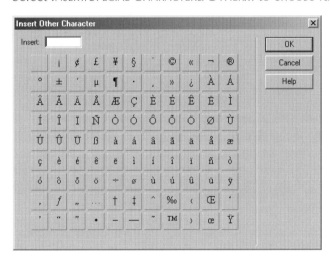

TIP

To place several empty spaces behind each other, select INSERT/SPECIAL CHARACTERS/NON BREAKING SPACE or press the Ctrl *+* ⇧ *+* ⬚ *keys. In the source code, a non breaking space will be saved as* .

If you would like to arrange a text area in columns, insert a table (see Chapter 6).

Find and replace

Seek and ye shall find... There are extensive search functions and options for replacing the words found by others in Dreamweaver.

You can determine the search: Dreamweaver can search for specific text areas, for text and tags in the HTML source code, for source code attributes or for complete tags.

1 Select EDIT/FIND AND REPLACE.

2 The dialog window FIND AND REPLACE opens.

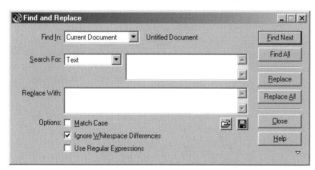

Depending on whether you are in the document window or the HTML view, the setting is different in the box SEARCH FOR.

Search for text:

1 Check the setting in the SEARCH FOR box. This must be set to TEXT.

2 If you would like to search through the current document, this must be chosen in the FIND IN box.

3 Enter the text which Dreamweaver is to search for in the large box beside it on the right. It can be a word, a sentence or just a few letters.

If you search for specific words, you should activate the check box MATCH CASE.

If you want to ignore differences in spacing, mark the corresponding option.

4 Click on FIND NEXT. If Dreamweaver finds a comparable text area, this will be displayed as highlighted in the current page. To be able to see the marking, you will probably need to move the search window.

5 If the text is not found, a corresponding message appears. Try again with another search string.

6 Click on CLOSE to close the window.

> **TIP**
>
> *You can search for documents all over the site or in a specific folder:*
>
> * *Mark the corresponding entry in the SEARCH FOR dialog box.*
> * *To search in a specific folder, you will first need to open it in the site window.*

To replace text:

1 Open the FIND AND REPLACE window with ⌃Ctrl + F.

2 Name the replacing text or source code. Make sure that you have the right setting under SEARCH FOR.

3 Name the new text or source code in the REPLACE WITH box.

4 Click on FIND NEXT.

5 If Dreamweaver has found a corresponding area, click on REPLACE.

6 To continue the controlled search, click on FIND NEXT.

Alternatively, click on REPLACE ALL if you wish Dreamweaver to replace all the occurrences matching the search criteria in the current document, the site or in a specific directory.

7 When you have finished, click on CLOSE.

CAUTION

Only use the REPLACE ALL button when you are really certain that Dreamweaver will replace the right areas. Be very careful – once this is completed, this action cannot be undone.

How to make a search through the whole site:

1 Mark the folder in the site window you want to search through.

2 Select EDIT/FIND AND REPLACE.

3 Click on the FIND ALL button. All the files will be searched according to the entered text area. A dialog window shows how many elements are found in how many files.

4 Click on OK. The results window that is displayed will list the occurring files if the elements appear. If you double click on a file in this list, this will be opened. The areas that are found are highlighted in the file.

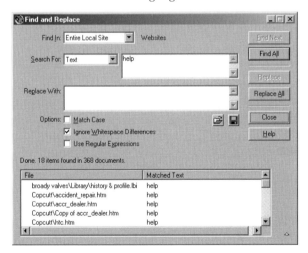

Straight to the point: shortcuts for the FIND AND REPLACE **function.**

	Windows	Macintosh
Find	Ctrl + F	⌘ + F
Replace	Ctrl + H	

Spell checking

In the Dreamweaver WYSIWYG editor, you can run a spell check on the whole document or just on a specific selection.

1 Select TEXT/CHECK SPELLING, or press ⇧ + F7.

2 As soon as Dreamweaver has found a word which does not appear in the dictionary, a corresponding message appears. The CHECK SPELLING dialog window appears.

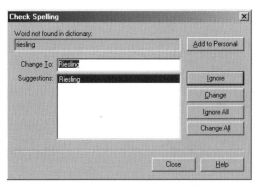

- If the word is spelt correctly, click on IGNORE.

- If the word is spelt correctly and you suspect it will occur several times on your page, click on IGNORE ALL.

- If the word is spelt wrongly, select the correct word from the list of suggestions or type it in the CHANGE box.

- If the word is spelt incorrectly and you suspect it will come up several more times on your page, write the correct spelling and click on CHANGE ALL.

3 When Dreamweaver has reached the end of the document, a dialog box appears:

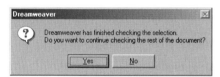

4 To be sure that the whole document has been thoroughly checked for spelling mistakes, you should continue the search.

5 When the search is complete, the above dialog window appears.

6 Confirm with OK.

Formatting paragraphs

In HTML, a paragraph is a text unit. Two paragraphs are separated by a larger gap. Therefore, a text unit is enclosed between <p> tags.

> **NOTE**
>
> *End a paragraph with </p>. Technically, this end tag is not required, as it has no further meaning. But to keep a cleaner programming style, and maintain a better overview of the HTML code, you should add it anyway.*

Normally, a text document is subdivided into several paragraphs. Because of this, single text blocks can be formatted in different ways. Headings, lists, subdivisions and pre-formatted text determine different types of paragraphs. It is also possible to format individual text parts (see previous chapter).

Creating a paragraph

1 Write the text. The line break is created automatically, as you well know from your word processing program.

2 To insert a paragraph, press ⏎.

The cursor jumps to the next line. A blank line was inserted after the previous paragraph.

Or:

1 Mark the text you want to merge into one paragraph.

2 In the Property Inspector, go to PARAGRAPH in the FORMAT drop-down menu.

The displayed document is structured in three paragraphs. It consists of a heading `<h1>` and two paragraphs enclosed in `<p>`. The text entered will be broken down automatically. In large text blocks, a linebreak `<br>` will be inserted.

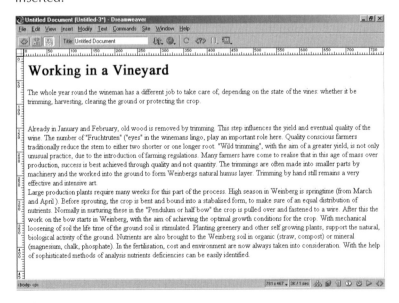

> **NOTE**
>
> *You get a single line break in a paragraph if you press* ⬆ *+* ⏎. *In the source code, <br> will be inserted. You can also call the special characters in the object panel and click on the <br> icon on the upper left.*

Assigning a paragraph format

HTML distinguishes between six different heading levels to represent hierarchy conditions. These can only be assigned to whole paragraphs, never to single words within a line.

<h1></h1> encloses the heading of the first level. Here, the text is displayed in the largest size.

<h6></h6>, on the other hand, defines the heading of level number six in the smallest size.

1 Click in a paragraph or mark several text blocks.

2 Select the desired formatting in the FORMAT drop-down menu in the Property Inspector:

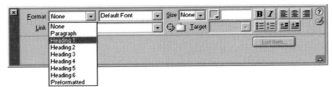

Or:

Select the desired format using the menu bar in the document window using TEXT/ PARAGRAPH FORMAT.

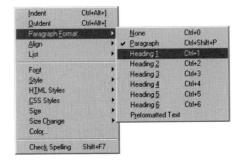

There are six hierarchical heading levels. Here you can see how the various headings are displayed.

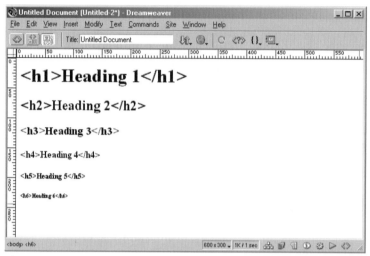

If you have created a text in another program and you would like to keep this appearance, you will need to save the text as PREFORMATTED TEXT in order to add it to your HTML page. Then the HTML conventions will not alter the text. For example, all the entered empty space characters will be after one another and line breaks will be kept.

1 In your document, click on the place where you want to insert the preformatted text.

2 Select TEXT/PARAGRAPH FORMAT/PREFORMATTED TEXT in the menu bar.

Or:

Select PREFORMATTED from the FORMAT drop-down menu in the Property Inspector.

The text goes on until you insert a line break with ⏎. Tabulators are also adopted. The basic structure of tables is kept. The text will be displayed in a default Monotype font (usually Courier or New Courier). Every character has the same width.

Lists

We distinguish between numbered lists, bulleted lists (unordered) and definition lists.

How to create an unordered list:

1 Enter the text. Set the paragraphs.

2 Mark the paragraphs.

3 Select TEXT/LIST/UNORDERED LIST from the menu bar.

Or:

Click on the  button in the Property Inspector.

The bullet points will be inserted in the list.

By default, round bullets will be used. You can choose to use square bullet points using Properties:

1 Right click in the paragraph and select LIST/PROPERTIES from the context menu. In the opening dialog box, you can now determine the numbering or the shape of the bullet points in the unordered list.

2 Confirm your details with OK.

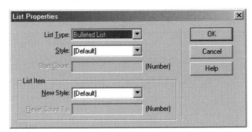

> **TIP**
>
> *Instead of the bullet points in the unordered list, you could insert graphics (see Chapter 4). Longer lists are best structured using tables (see Chapter 6).*

How to create an ordered list:

1 Mark the paragraph.

2 Click on the ▤ button in the Property Inspector or select TEXT/LIST/ORDERED LIST from the menu bar.

If you remove a bullet point from the list, the remaining ones will be renumbered:

To add a new item to the list, click at the end of the previous bullet point text. Click on ⏎. The ordered list will be extended with a new numbered item.

The procedure is the same with all lists.

How to create a definition list:

1 Enter the text. Create the paragraphs.

2 Mark the paragraphs.

3 Select TEXT/LIST/DEFINITION LIST from the menu bar.

A definition list contains, on the one hand, the term defined as <dt>, and, on the other, the indented definition <dd>. You can also format the text further.

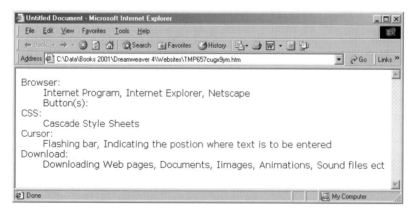

NOTE

As an alternative to the definition list, you could use the ▣ ▣ buttons in the Property Inspector. With these, you can also indent paragraphs.

TIPS

- To create a normal paragraph from a list, click on the corresponding list buttons (▣, ▣) in the Property Inspector, or click on ▣.

- You can structure lists with the ▣ ▣ buttons in the Property Inspector without having to use list symbols.

- You can quickly create an unordered list (and vice versa) from an ordered list by clicking on the corresponding list buttons in the Property Inspector. This, of course, works on definition lists as well. However, to do this, you will have to work over the TEXT/LIST/ DEFINITION LIST in the menu bar.

- To finish list formatting, press twice on ⏎.

- If you have problems when creating a list, check whether both the opening paragraph tag <p> and the end tag </p> are present.

Aligning paragraphs

Text, paragraphs, lists or the whole page can either be aligned to the left, to the right or centred in your document.

1 Mark the text for which you want to change the alignment.

2 Click on the corresponding buttons in the Property Inspector:
▣ ▣ ▣
or
use the menu TEXT/ALIGN and then LEFT, RIGHT or CENTRE. The text will be aligned accordingly.

By default, the text will be aligned to the left. There is no need to use any special settings for this.

The command for text alignment can be enclosed in different tags. Some examples:

```
<p align=«center«></p>
```

```
<div align="center"></div>
```

```
<h1 align=«center«></h1>
```

The formatting stops simultaneously with the end tag.

You can align whole text blocks, but not just a part of a heading or a paragraph.

Other elements, such as images or tables, can be aligned in similar ways. You will learn more about this in the corresponding chapters.

Create text indents:

As briefly described in the last chapter, you could indent text paths in definition lists. You have another option of using the `<blockquote></blockquote>` tag.

1 Click on the paragraph you would like to indent. If you would like to assign more than one indent, mark all these paragraphs.

2 Select TEXT/INDENT from the menu bar to indent the text one unit to the right, or TEXT/OUTDENT to move the text one unit to the left.

Or:

Use the icons in the Property Inspector. With the ⊞ button, you move the paragraph one unit to the left, by pressing the ⊞ button you move it one unit to the right.

Or:

Use the following shortcuts:

[Ctrl] + [Alt] + [9]   Indent

[Ctrl] + [Alt] + [8]   Outdent

Repeat these steps until the text is in the desired place.

> **CAUTION**
>
> *You can arrange several <blockquote> tags behind each other. The outdent respectively eliminates the <blockquote>. In doing so, you remove one indent unit. Therefore, this command works only if you have already made an indentation.*

In the following example, the second paragraph is indented by several <blockquote> units. As a result, the paragraph is indented both from the left and from the right:

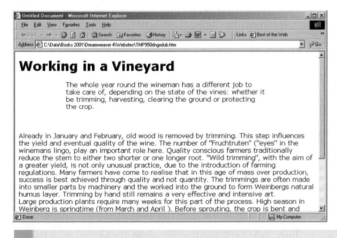

> **TIP**
>
> *Tables gives another option: setting borders (see Chapter 6).*

Horizontal rules

It is very easy to separate your text into different sections with a horizontal rule.

How to build a horizontal rule:

1 In your document, click where you want to insert the line.

2 Select INSERT/HORIZONTAL RULE in the menu bar.

Or press the ▦ button in the Object manager in the COMMON panel.

> **NOTE**
>
> *This inserted horizontal rule is not formatted yet. It has the default values "whole width", "centered" and "3D shading".*

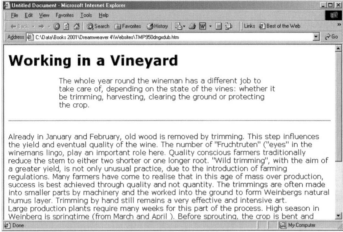

You can change the properties of the rule:

1 Mark the horizontal rule. You can see the set characteristics in the Property Inspector.

If this is not open, double click on the horizontal line.

2 Enter the name of the rule in the text box.

3 Determine the width. You enter this either in pixels or as a percentage of the window width. Then you enter the measurement unit in the drop-down menu.

4 Determine the height in pixels.

5 You determine the alignment by using the corresponding drop-down menu.

6 To remove the shade, deactivate the SHADING check box.

> **NOTE**
>
> *The Web browser centres a division line by default. However, the alignment only occurs in relation to the instruction* width, *with which you shorten the division line, since otherwise the division line covers the whole width of the display window.*

> **TIP**
>
> *To get coloured division lines, name the* color *attribute as a hex value in the code. In doing so, you determine the colour of the division line. However, this is only shown in Microsoft Internet Explorer version 3.0 and higher.*

HTML tags

Dreamweaver is a WYSIWYG editor. This means that you can develop an HTML page without having any knowledge of HTML. Of course, if you have this knowledge, I am not complaining. The fact that you know HTML will make it easier for you to understand what Dreamweaver does in the background, for example in the HTML editor.

As already mentioned, HTML is the leading language on the Web. The abbreviation stands for **H**yper **T**ext **M**arkup **L**anguage. HTML is a description language, which is then translated into an optical image in the browser.

> **NOTE**
>
> *HTML is not a programming language. HTML contains no loops, no if statements, or any other function which label a classical programming language.*

You have already heard something about HTML in the previous chapters. In this one, we would like to introduce more secrets of this language. You will see that HTML is not difficult, thanks to its logical construction.

The HTML Source Inspector

You already know that HTML pages consist of various tags, which mark page elements in order to format them, and to align and insert links and instructions.

Most tags consist of two tags, a start and an end tag.

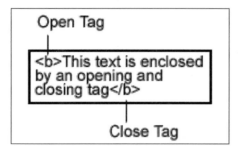

This text will later be displayed in bold in the Web browser. This is determined by the <b> tag, which encloses the text to be formatted. Start and end tags are not visible in the Web browser, and appear only in the source code.

> **TIP**
>
> *Keep the HTML Source Inspector open when editing and formatting an HTML document. Then you can monitor how your work in the document window affects the source code. You can easily learn HTML in this way.*

You can apply even more formatting to a page element. The different tags are encapsulated in a corresponding order.

If additional formatting is carried out simultaneously, the tags are encapsulated in a specific order:

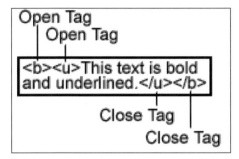

The start and the end <u> tag stand next to the text. The <b> tag is above this. Tags encapsulate the document elements to be formatted from the inside to the outside.

It becomes more confusing if, for example, we have a table, consisting of one cell, with text that is linked to a Web site, but which, at the same time, should be displayed in a particular font and font size.

```
          Open Tag
<table width="100%" border="0" hieght="250">
  <tr>
    <td><font face="Arial, Helvetica, sans-serif" size="3">Copyright
    &copy; 2001 by <a href="http://www.cybertechnics.co.uk">Cybertechnics</a>
</font></td>
  </tr>
</table> —— Close Tag                          Formated Text
```

At first, the browser is informed that a <table> table of a certain size (width, height) follows. The first row is then defined (<tr> stands for table row), followed by the table cell (<td> means table data). In this tag, only the cell content is enclosed. The <font> tag encapsulates the whole text and determines the font and the font size. The link is defined with the anchor tag <a href></a>. The text placed between these two tags carries a link.

This is how the entered source code looks in the Dreamweaver document window and later on in the Web browser:

Copyright © 2001 by Cybertechnics

> **NOTE**
>
> *You will find more information about how to construct a table in Chapter 6.*

Unfortunately, you cannot begin with the formatting. An HTML document must contain some general tags.

You will see in the HTML Source Inspector that when you create an empty HTML document, Dreamweaver uses the same tag layout. An HTML page has the following structure:

```
<html>
<head>
<title></title>
</head>

<body>

</body>
</html>
```

You define the document as a Web document using the `<html>` tag. There are two areas: the document head is enclosed by `<head>` tags, the document body is determined by the `<body>` tags. Specific tags are used within both of these areas.

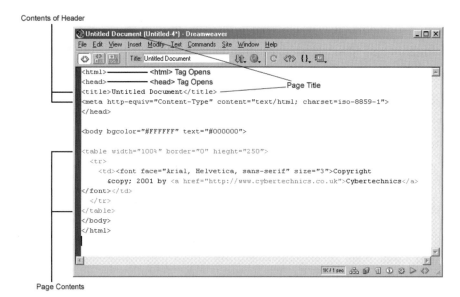

TIP

You are able to look at the HTML coding for every Web page. Right click in the Web browser. Select VIEW SOURCE from the context menu that opens up.

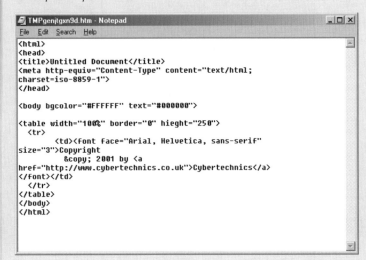

```
<html>
<head>
<title>Untitled Document</title>
<meta http-equiv="Content-Type" content="text/html;
charset=iso-8859-1">
</head>

<body bgcolor="#FFFFFF" text="#000000">

<table width="100%" border="0" hieght="250">
  <tr>
      <td><Font face="Arial, Helvetica, sans-serif"
size="3">Copyright
          &copy; 2001 by <a
href="http://www.cybertechnics.co.uk">Cybertechnics</a>
</Font></td>
    </tr>
</table>
</body>
</html>
```

Tag	Name	Use	Start and end tag
<html>	HTML	Document	yes
<head>	Head	Document	yes
<title>	Page title	Document	yes
<body>*	Body	Document	yes
<h1>...<h6>	Heading	Paragraph	yes
<p>	Paragraph	Paragraph	yes/no (not absolutely necessary)
 	Line break	Text	no
<blockquote>	Quotation	Paragraph	yes/no (not absolutely necessary)

Tag	Name	Use	Start and end tag
`<ul>`	List (unordered)	Paragraph, list	yes/no (not absolutely necessary)
`<ol>`	List (ordered)	Paragraph, list	yes
`<li>`	List entry	Paragraph, list	no
`<dl>`	Definition list	Paragraph, list	yes
`<dt><dd>`	Expression, definition of expression	Paragraph, list	yes
`<center>`	Centre	Paragraph	yes/no (not absolutely necessary)
`<b>`	Bold	Paragraph, text block	yes
`<i>`	Italic	Text, text block	yes
`<u>`	Underline	Text, text block	yes
`<font>*`	Font	Text, text block	yes
`<img>*`	Image	Image	no
`<a>*`	Anchor, hyperlink	Text, text block, paragraph	yes
`<table>*`	Table	Table	yes
`<tr>`	Table row	Table	yes
`<td>`	Table cell	Table	yes
`<frameset>*`	Definition of frameset	Document	yes
`<frame>*`	Definition of frame	Document	yes
`<form>*`	Form	Form	yes
`<input>*`	Form box	Form	no
`<select>*`	Selection menu	Form	yes

*Table 3.1: Overview of the most important and most frequently used HTML tags. HTML control commands dealing with attributes are marked with * . It is often possible to derive the command from the tag name*

Tag	Example	Description
`<body>*`	`<body bgcolor="#FFFFFF" text="#000000" link="CC0000" leftmargin="35">`	Background colour=white, text=black, links=red, left margin=35 Pixels
`<font>*`	`<font face="arial" size="3" colour="#CC0000">`	Font=Arial, font size=3, font colour=red
`<img>*`	`<img src="bild/ fallschirm.jpg" width="163" height="223">`	Image name, directory, image size (width, height)
`<a>*`	`<a href="home.htm" target="_top">`	The target file (home.htm) should be displayed in the whole of the browser window
`<table>*`	`<table width="75%" border="1">`	The table width is 75% of the screen width, borders=1 Pixel

Table 3.2: A few examples of tags and attributes

TIP

You could activate the row numbers in the Options menu to obtain a better overview of the document window. The line break is also very useful if you have long rows.

Set the different views in the Options menu to the right in the HTML Source Inspector:

103

How to use the Quick Tag Editor:

1 Open the QUICK TAG EDITOR by clicking on the pencil icon in the Property Inspector.

2 Enter a tag. If you pause in typing, this pop-up menu appears, where you can select more tags and attributes.

The Tag Selector

You are able to mark and edit all tags via the Dreamweaver status bar. According to what is marked in the document, or where the pointer is placed, the Tag Selector shows different HTML areas.

Click on the tag you would like to edit. The page elements that these control commands enclose are now marked both in the document window and in the HTML Source Inspector.

To mark a cell, for example, click inside it and select the Tag Selector `<td>`. You could also select a row `<tr>` or the whole table `<table>`.

> **NOTE**
>
> *You can mark the whole document any time. For this, click on* `<body>`*. This tag is always visible in the Tag Selector.*

Right click on a tag in the Tag Selector. In the menu that opens up you can, for example, remove and edit the tag.

Comments

You can insert notes to document your Web page. These comments only appear in the source code. Here you can, for example, type in where a table starts and ends, when and which alterations are made, or how a complex JavaScript is built up.

Comments always have the following shape:

```
<! -- I am invisible in the browser.-->
```

1 To enter a comment, select INSERT/INVISIBLE TAGS/COMMENT. The INSERT COMMENT dialog window appears.

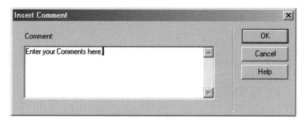

2 Enter your comment here.

TIP

You open a comment in the document window by clicking on the 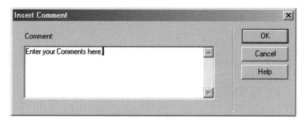 *icon. If this is not visible, you will need to go to EDIT/PREFERENCES >INVISIBLE ELEMENTS to activate it.*

Determine the structure of the source code in Preferences.

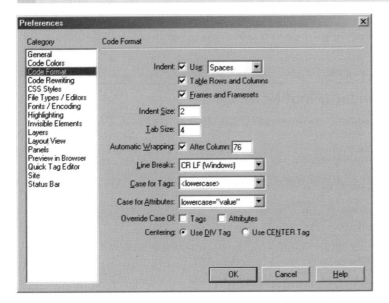

Cleaning up HTML

Mainly files from other programs or hand-coded HTML documents consist partly of incorrect source code. These incorrect tags will be visible in the document window and can easily be deleted or corrected.

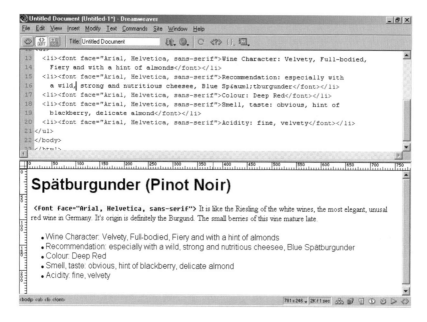

Even if you open a faulty file in Dreamweaver, the errors will automatically be corrected. Therefore, the corresponding check box is, by default, activated in Preferences under CODE REWRITING.

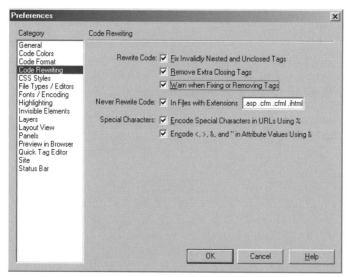

Adjust it so that a pop-up window appears with a message describing the errors that have been automatically corrected:

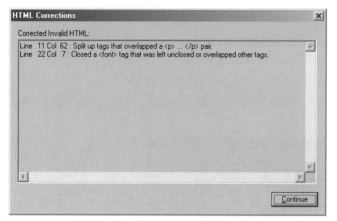

You can carry out further clean-ups of the source code at any time:

1 Select COMMANDS/CLEAN UP HTML.

2 In the CLEAN UP HTML window that opens, activate which errors should be eliminated. Mark the corresponding check boxes for this.

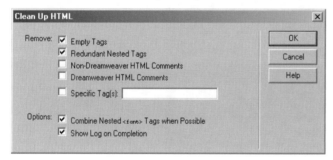

3 Confirm your selection with OK.

TIP

Dreamweaver also produces superfluous source code. Therefore, activate COMBINE NESTED <font> TAGS when possible in the CLEAN UP HTML window. To see which errors Dreamweaver has eliminated, activate the SHOW LOG ON COMPLETION check box.

If you import a text file from Word, this will partly contain bad errors, which Dreamweaver can recognise and in most cases clean up.

1 In Dreamweaver, open the Word document saved as an HTML file.

2 Select COMMANDS/CLEAN UP WORD HTML in the menu bar.

Dreamweaver now "scans" the HTML document to identify the Word version with which it was created.

When Dreamweaver is not able to determine the Word version automatically, the following message appears:

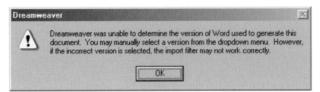

3 Click on OK and then select the underlying version in the CLEAN UP WORD HTML dialog box.

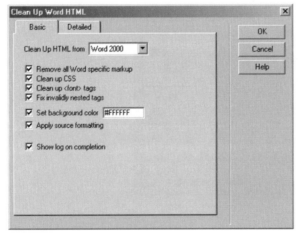

In addition, you will see the modifications Dreamweaver can perform on the document. This dialog window will look a little different, depending on the Word version identified.

4 Click on OK. Dreamweaver now revises the document after the adjustments you have made. A log is then displayed if you have activated the corresponding check box.

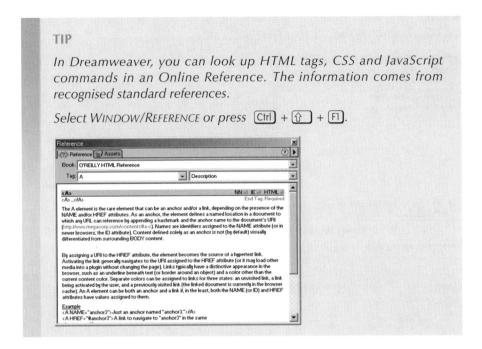

HTML Styles

Sometimes, it can be quite bothersome to have to keep on creating the same formatting. It is then pleasant to discover that if you want all <h1> headings to be in bold, italic and green, you can save this as an HTML Style and use it for all of your HTML documents on your Web site.

WHAT IS THIS?

*An **HTML Style** is a formatting catalogue, which you can save, modify and delete. Several tags and attributes are combined in this catalogue to format a text or a paragraph. If you use certain combinations of formatting over and over again, it will definitely be quicker to automate these work steps. In order to do this, make use of the HTML Style panel.*

How to open the HTML Style panel:

Click on the button in the Launcher bar or in the Mini-Launcher.

Alternatively, you can select WINDOW/HTML STYLES in the menu bar. Or use the corresponding shortcut $\boxed{Ctrl}$ + $\boxed{F11}$.

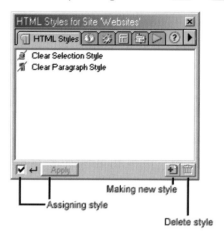

Making new style
Assigning style
Delete style

> **TIP**
>
> *With the help of the HTML Style panel palette, you can save the HTML Style which is employed on a site and then use it together with other users on local or remote sites.*

How to create a new HTML Style on the basis of existing text:

1 In the document, select the text area on which the new HTML Style should base its formatting.

2 Click on the NEW STYLE symbol in the HTML Style panel.

3 Name the style in the DEFINE HTML STYLE dialog box.

4 Check the determined formatting.

5 Determine whether you would like to apply the style to the paragraph or to a text passage.

6 Define whether the available style should be replaced, or whether you want to apply the new style as well.

How to create a completely new HTML Style:

1 Click on the NEW STYLE ☰ symbol in the HTML Style panel. You can also select TEXT/HTML STYLE/NEW STYLE, or work with the context menu.

2 Carry out steps 3 and 4 described in the instructions for how to make a new style based on existing text.

3 Click on OK.

How to use an existing HTML Style:

1 Mark the text or the paragraph you want to format.

2 Select a style from the HTML Style panel.

CAUTION

You can only use CLEAR SELECTION STYLE and CLEAR PARAGRAPH STYLE on text where there is already a style applied. These two entries in the HTML Style panel are not styles and can neither be displayed nor edited.

1 If the APPLY check box is activated in the panel, click once on a style. The selected style will then automatically be applied.

2 If the check box is deactivated, click on the style and then on APPLY.

3 The selected text or paragraph is now formatted.

How to establish new settings for an existing HTML Style:

1 Double click on the HTML Style.

2 Establish the settings for the style in the DEFINE HTML STYLE window.

You determine with the APPLY TO option whether the style should be applied to the selected text (SELECTION) or to the current text block (PARAGRAPH).

After this, you can decide with the options below whether you want to add the style to the existing one (ADD TO EXISTING STYLE) or clear the existing style and replace it with the new settings (CLEAR EXISTING STYLE).

3 Confirm your alterations with OK.

How to establish a new HTML Style on the basis of an existing HTML Style:

1 Right click (Windows) or press the Ctrl key (Macintosh) on a similar style in the Style panel.

> CAUTION
>
> *Make sure that no text is selected in the document.*

2 Select the DUPLICATE option in the context menu. The DEFINE HTML STYLE dialog box appears.

3 Give the new style a name and define the properties.

4 Confirm with OK.

How to clear text formatting in a document:

1 Select the formatted text.

2 Click on CLEAR SELECTION STYLE or CLEAR PARAGRAPH STYLE in the HTML Style panel.

With the CLEAR SELECTION STYLE you remove all formatting from the selected text. If you would like to remove the formatting from the whole paragraph, select CLEAR PARAGRAPH STYLE.

How to remove a style from the HTML Style panel:

1 Deactivate the APPLY check box in the HTML Style panel.

2 Select an HTML Style.

3 Click on the DELETE STYLE (waste basket) symbol.

Chapter 4

Working with images

An image speaks louder than a thousand words. Keep this message in your heart, because the visual medium of the Internet definitely requires attractive and interesting images. Underline the message your site is aiming to convey with matching photos and graphics. This is often a balancing act, because any attached image will increase the loading time of the Web page. In this chapter, we will show the options Dreamweaver offers when inserting and editing images. In addition, you will learn how to obtain special effects with simple functions.

The Internet has been a visual medium since 1994. Prior to that, it was not possible to view images online in a browser. If an image was to be used, it had to be downloaded and then viewed offline. This was not only time consuming but also very haphazard.

Inserting images

You have already seen how to install an image in the background, in Chapter 2. In this workshop, you will learn how to integrate an image in the foreground, which means placing it in the actual HTML document. Here are several ways to do it:

1 In the document, click on where you want to insert the image:

2 Press the INSERT IMAGE 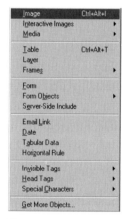 button in the object palette.

Or:

Select INSERT/IMAGE in the menu bar.

Image	Ctrl+Alt+I
Interactive Images	▶
Media	▶
Table	Ctrl+Alt+T
Layer	
Frames	▶
Form	
Form Objects	▶
Server-Side Include	
Email Link	
Date	
Tabular Data	
Horizontal Rule	
Invisible Tags	▶
Head Tags	▶
Special Characters	▶
Get More Objects...	

Or:

Press (Ctrl) + (Alt) + (Del).

3 Select the directory and the filename of the image in the SELECT IMAGE SOURCE dialog box that opens.

The name of the image appears in the FILE NAME text box. In addition, you can view a preview of the image that also states its height and width, file size and download time.

If you already know the URL, enter it now directly into the text field.

4 Click on SELECT. The dialog box closes and the image appears in the document window.

In case you want to insert an image into an HTML file which has not yet been saved, this dialog box appears:

Click on OK. In Chapter 2 you can find out how to save a file and create a local site.

How to select an image:

You need to select an image to work with it. For this purpose, click on the image. A "handle" appears in the lower right hand corner.

Now you can edit, copy and cut out the image. These commands are found in the menu bar under EDIT, or you can use the shortcuts you already know (see the shortcuts list in the Appendix).

It is also possible to alter the image properties (see Image properties on page 121) or replace it with another image.

The image becomes unselected if you click on a different place in the actual document.

To select several images, drag the cursor over them while holding down the mouse button. Alternatively, click on the images one by one, while pressing the ⇧ key. The images will then appear in grey and no longer have "handles".

Image formats

Most Web browsers display the **GIF** and **JPG** or **JPEG** image formats. In addition, fourth generation browsers (including Dreamweaver 4) support the **PNG** format.

If your images are in a different format from one of the three described, you will need to convert them:

1 Open the photo or the graphic in an image editing program (such as Fireworks, Photoshop).

2 Usually you will find the entry for FILE/SAVE AS or FILE/EXPORT in the menu bar of your image editing program. Determine the file type in the dialog window that opens.

3 You then determine the directory and the file name. Confirm with OK.

You will find further information in Help and in the manual of your image editing program.

Well, what is the best format?

JPGs support millions of colours and therefore can represent many details. However, colour information is lost in the compression. The more you compress a JPG, the smaller the file size becomes, but at the same time, you keep losing more and more colours. The image becomes less sharp and pixelated.

The **GIF** format was developed by CompuServe. With this, you are able to save only 256 colours. These colours are not predefined. However, there are so-called Web safe colours (more information about this can be found in Chapter 2, under Page properties). In addition to this, you can create transparent GIFs in your image editing program. In doing so, you determine which colours should disappear. Parts of the transparent GIF will in this way appear more strongly integrated into the background.

JPG should be used for photos and graphics with continuous hues. GIFs are suitable for pictures with large areas of similar colour and grey scale pictures. In addition, you can create animations.

The new **PNG** image format offers considerably more options than the GIF and JPG formats. It supports index colours, grey scale and true colour images, as well as the alpha channel and the representation of transparency. There is just as little loss of quality through compression as there is loss of definite number of colours. Unfortunately, at the moment only a few browsers (among others IE and NN version 4) can interpret this image format.

> **NOTE**
>
> *Images increase the loading time of a Web site. As a rule, the user can access the other pages on your Internet presence from the home page. Pay attention to the loading time of this page. When loading time is too long, many users will stop the loading and move on to surf somewhere else.*

Image properties

To be able to see the images in the Property Inspector, click once on the corresponding image.

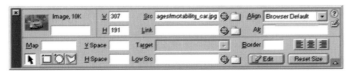

If the Property Inspector is not open, open it using WINDOW/PROPERTIES (see Chapter 1).

The Property Inspector shows the single image features, as well as the miniature, thumbnail view. Here you can, for example, alter an image height and width, install links (see Chapter 5), determine the orientation of the image, or define a border.

TIP

Give your image a sensible name. Use the name when you want to work with JavaScript. The name will not appear in the browser.

Naming an image:

1 Select the image.

2 Enter a name for the image in the Property Inspector.

3 Press ⏎.

Or, click on the APPLY button, which in this case is a miniature view of the image.

You will now only see the name in the source code.

CAUTION

Only use small letters for the image name, and no blank spaces or special characters.

Assigning an ALT text:

Not everybody uses the option of the image display. You should use the ALT attribute to give people the message of the image. On this occasion ALT stands for alternative text.

1 Select the image.

2 Write the alternative text in the ALT text field in the Property Inspector.

3 Press ↵ or click on the APPLY button.

Users see this dummy if they have turned off the display in their browser:

Müller- Thurgau

☒ The Müller-Thurgau grape

The most cultivated wine region in Germany (24%). It was first cultivated by 1882 by Professor H. Müller in Geisenheim. It is most probably a cross between the Riesling and Sylvaner grapes. The berries usually reach full maturity by the end of September.

Colour: pale-bright yellow

Character: delicate, muscatel aroma, milder in acidity than the Riesling

Acidity: very mild

Body, content: average to firm

Recommendation: Drink fresh and young - with dishes neutral and delicate in aroma. Storage life should not exceed three years.

Several browsers will show an information box if you move the mouse over an image:

Müller- Thurgau

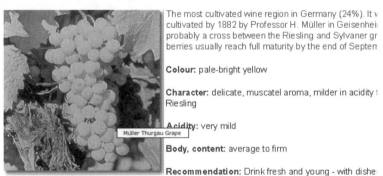

The most cultivated wine region in Germany (24%). It v cultivated by 1882 by Professor H. Müller in Geisenhei probably a cross between the Riesling and Sylvaner gr berries usually reach full maturity by the end of Septen

Colour: pale-bright yellow

Character: delicate, muscatel aroma, milder in acidity Riesling

Acidity: very mild

Müller Thurgau Grape

Body, content: average to firm

Recommendation: Drink fresh and young - with dishe: delicate in aroma. Storage life should not exceed three years.

Images with a lower resolution

Very large images (from about 30 KB) take a correspondingly longer loading time. To overcome this waiting period, you can define a low resolution image as a preliminary dummy on your Web page for the high quality image. This will be displayed only until the right image is in place.

1 Select the high quality image already inserted.

2 Enter the source of the image which should be displayed first in the LOW SRC text box in the Property Inspector.

You can either key this in directly or click on the SEARCH button 🔲 beside it and select the image source from the now opening dialog window.

Or use the POINT TO FILE 🎯 option.

3 Confirm your input with ⏎ or click on the APPLY button.

The image on the left is 2 KB, the one on the right is 30 KB. The left source image is immediately visible and is displayed until the right one appears.

> CAUTION
>
> *The image with the low resolution must have the same dimensions as the main image.*

To define a border of the image:

By default, Dreamweaver displays all images without borders. You can define the border thickness yourself.

1 Select the image that should be given a border.

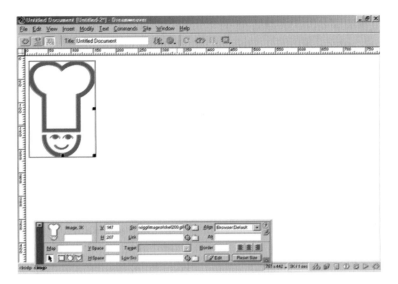

2 Define the frame border in pixels. To be able to see the BORDER text box, you will need to open the extended view of the Property Inspector.

Border 5

3 Press ⏎ or click on the APPLY button. A border now surrounds the image. The image is still the same. The border is defined by the HTML source code `border="5"`.

NOTE

By default, the border colour is black. If the image is linked, the frame will be displayed in the link colour.

Enlarging or reducing

When you insert an image in the Dreamweaver document, it will appear in the size it was saved in.

You can very simply alter this size in the Property Inspector:

1 Select the image for which you wish to change the size.

2 Pull the picture at the "handles" to the desired size. The new scaling is taken into the Property Inspector.

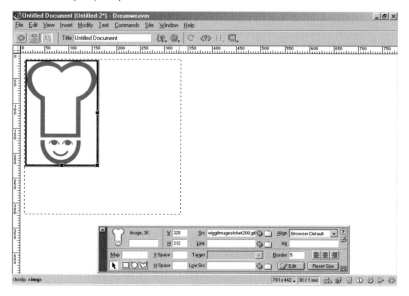

Alternatively, enter the size in the height and the width text boxes in the Property Inspector. You can enter the new measurements in centimetres, millimetres, inches, picas or points. In order to do this, you will need to key in the values in the measurement unit. Make sure that no empty space is left between the value and the measurement unit. If you do not name a unit, Dreamweaver scales in pixels. Dreamweaver also changes all other values into pixels.

If the new values do not correspond to the size of the saved picture, these appear bold in the Property Inspector.

3 Confirm with ⏎ or click on the APPLY button. In this example, the image width is extended.

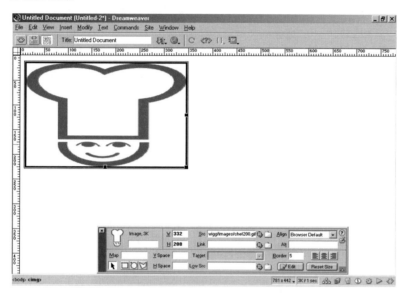

NOTE

If the browser recognises the image and its given size, a field for the image will be kept free while it is being loaded.

WHAT IS THIS?

*When you alter the height or width of an image or another page element, you are **scaling** it.*

Positioning images

When aligning text, you had the choice between aligning left, right or centre. Even more options are available with images.

1 Select the image you would like to align.

2 Determine the desired position in the Property Inspector. For this, use the ALIGN drop-down menu.

CAUTION

Some positions are only visible when they are viewed with other objects (see Figure 4.1: the attribute is shown against the image of the house. The option is either to align it with other images or with some text).

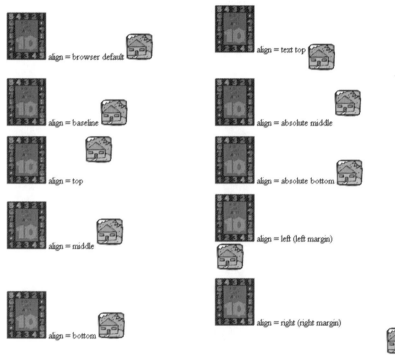

Figure 4.1: The attribute is shown against the image of the house. The option is either to align it with other images or with some text

An inserted image may "stick" to another image, or directly to a text. In the following example, all the images were inserted behind each other. In this case, Dreamweaver automatically inserts blank characters. I have removed these in the second line of code.

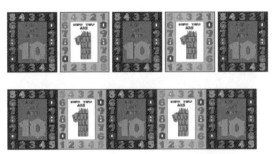

To achieve more distance between individual image elements, you will need to define both a horizontal and a vertical blank space surrounding the actual image:

1 Select the images that should have more distance from the other surrounding elements.

2 Enter the desired distance in pixels into the text box's V space (vertical) and H space (horizontal).

3 Press ⏎ or click on the APPLY button. Now a surrounding space is entered for the image.

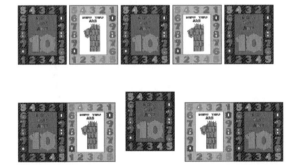

The surrounding spacing is defined for the third image in the second row. This is 15 pixels, both horizontally and vertically. This space influences the complete line. The space between the images in the previous row is larger.

> **NOTE**
>
> *If the images overlap, just put them into different layers (see Chapter 9).*

Working with external image editors

To create and modify images for your site, you can work on your images in an external graphical program. Generally speaking, you can use whatever graphics program you like.

However, the integration of Macromedia Fireworks 4 is recommended for effective work. The same tools and commands are, to a large extent, available in both programs. This allows for efficient, simple and common images and HTML editing. In Fireworks you can, for example, integrate and edit created, Web-optimised images and HTML files for your Dreamweaver document. Vice versa, you can change a graphic in Fireworks and then automatically update it in the open HTML document.

In PREFERENCES (in the menu bar under Edit) you can set up an external graphics program for image editing. Fireworks is particularly well suited for this purpose.

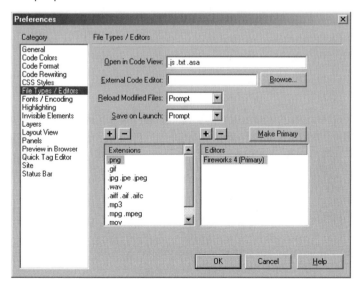

How to integrate new editors in Dreamweaver:

1 Select EDIT/PREFERENCES from the menu bar.

2 Click on the FILE TYPES/EDITORS category.

3 Select the file type you would like to work with in the integrated editor.

4 Then click on (+) in the list of editors.

5 Select the desired application from the dialog box.

6 This selected application can be defined as a primary editor for these file types.

7 Confirm with OK.

To delete an editor from the list, click on (–).

NOTE

- *In the settings, the graphic program must be listed as the first editor (see below).*

- *If you are working with a team of people on a Web site, you should save your comments in DESIGN NOTES. These notes appear neither in the browser nor in the source code. Select FILE/DESIGN NOTES in the menu bar. The design notes are marked with ⬚ in the site window.*

TIP

You optimise an image in Fireworks when you give this command in Dreamweaver: highlight the image and select COMMANDS/OPTIMIZE IMAGE IN FIREWORKS.

How to open the external editor:

- Double clicking on the image you want to edit will start the external editor.

- Double click on the image file in the site window.

> **TIP**
>
> *At first, a dialog window appears in Fireworks, asking you whether you would like to edit the graphic integrated on the Web page or work on the original file.*

Creating rollovers

In Dreamweaver you have the option of creating an effective rollover effect. With such an effect, images will, if you move your mouse over them, be replaced. If you then leave the image area, the original image can be seen again.

Rollovers are often used for buttons. When you move the mouse over a button, this is highlighted or appears in another shape.

You can make funny rollover effects with all kinds of images:

How to create a simple rollover image:

1 Select INSERT/INTERACTIVE IMAGES/ROLLOVER IMAGE from the menu bar.

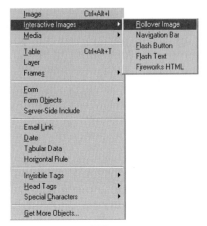

Or click on the 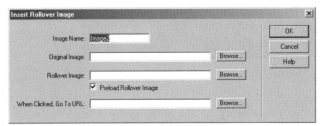 button in the Object panel.

2 The dialog window INSERT ROLLOVER IMAGE appears.

Here you give the directory and filename of the original image and the rollover image.

3 Activate the preload rollover image check box. Otherwise, there would be an unnecessary waiting time, which would ruin the rollover effect.

4 If you would like to link your image to a Web page, name the URL or click on the BROWSE button (you will find further information about hyperlinks in Chapter 5).

5 Click on OK to insert the rollover on your page.

TIP

You could define rollover images in *INSERT/INTERACTIVE IMAGES/
NAVIGATION BAR*. More information about this is to be found in
Chapter 10. Here, you will learn more about JavaScript and
behaviours.

TIP

As the rollover image adapts to the size of the original image, all
images should have the same size.

CAUTION

Test the rollover in a browser capable of interpreting JavaScript.

Creating image maps

What is this?

An **image map** is an image divided up into single image areas (hotspots). These
hotspots are respectively linked to various pages.

How to create an image map:

1 Select the image.

2 Enter the name of the MAP in the MAP text box.

To see these settings, you will need to click on the expanding arrow.

3 Click on the circle, the rectangle or the polygon. Drag the pointer onto the
image. To create a polygon, click once for every corner point.

4 To determine the properties of a hotspot, highlight it:

135

If you cannot see the hotspot, the image is no longer selected.

5 Set the features of this hotspot in the Property Inspector:

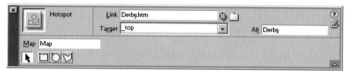

Define the page the user will get to if he/she clicks on this place. You will read more about links in Chapter 5.

6 Enter the alternative text in the ALT box.

7 Repeat the steps to lay out further hotspots or to define their features.

> **TIP**
>
> *To change the position or the size of a hotspot afterwards, highlight it and move the "handles" with the arrow tool in the Property Inspector. You can then form a new polygon.*

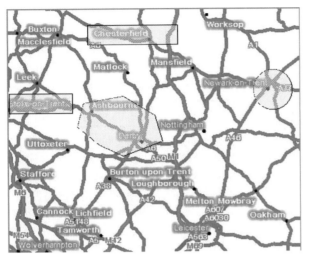

This map contains four hotspots altogether. These are only deposited in colour in Dreamweaver. If you move your mouse over such an area in the browser, you will see that there is a link. Mark the hotspot to be able to determine the features.

NOTE

- If you create several image maps, make sure that you give every map a clear name.

- If you would like to copy an image with hotspots, first mark the real image. Then press the ⬆ button and click on every single hotspot. You can now copy the highlighted elements into the intermediate file and insert them in the same document, or in another document.

Chapter 5

Hyperlinks

In this chapter, you will see how simple it is to install hyperlinks on your Web page. You will be able to create links to other documents within your Web site, an external link to your favourite Web site on the WWW, or a link to an e-mail. To jump to a definite place in your document, we use named anchors. In conclusion, I will show you how quickly and simply you can manage your links in Dreamweaver.

Inserting hyperlinks

How to insert a relative (internal) link:

1 Highlight the element (such as text or image) you wish to link.

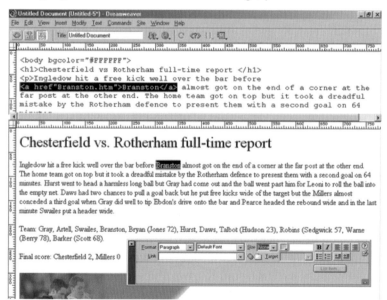

2 Enter the directory and file name of the target Web site in the HYPERLINK text box in the Property Inspector.

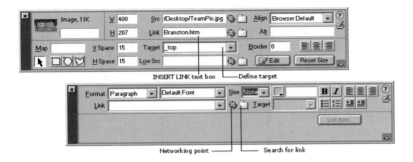

INSERT LINK text box ———| |—Define target

Networking point ——— |— Search for link

If it is a link on a Web page within the same Web site, you could also select the file using the folder icon 🗀. Then the SELECT FILE dialog window opens.

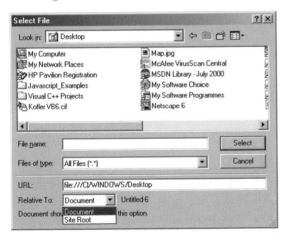

Search your hard drive as normal and then highlight the file found. In the drop-down menu, select either DOCUMENT, to produce a relative path, or SITE ROOT, for a central position in your Web page.

Alternatively, use `point to file` 🌐 and drag it to the target file in the site window while holding down the mouse button.

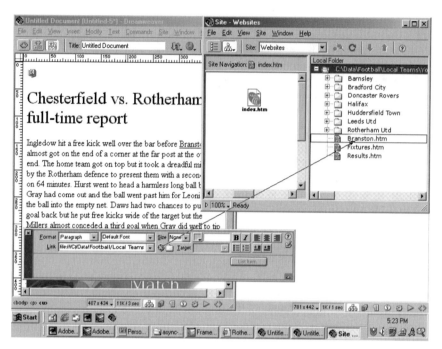

3 Press ⏎.

WHAT IS THIS?

Relative links *refers to other documents in the same site* (`../`
`internet/index.htm`). *In the example above, we are looking at a*
relative instruction.

Absolute links *gives the complete path* (`http://`
`www.intermedia.net/index.htm`).

Root relative path names (`/index.htm`) *refer to a document in the*
same site. The server directory forms the basis here. This kind of link is
mainly suitable for large sites, where the files are frequently moved
around.

Named anchor *is connected to a definite point in the same document*
or to a definite place on another page (`#top` *or* `../`
`index.htm#top`).

How to move hyperlinks in the site window:

1 Activate the MAP AND FILES view as you click on the 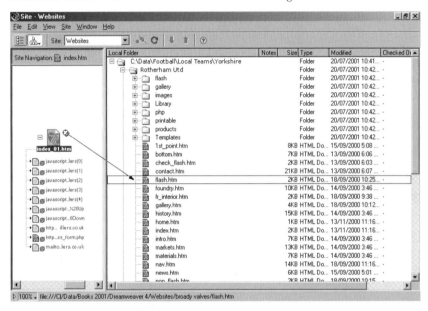 button in the site window and wait while holding down the mouse button, until the drop-down menu appears with this option.

2 In the left column, you can see the visual representation of the site, with all the links. The directories and the files are listed on the right.

3 In the left column, highlight the document to which you want to create a new link. The point to file appears.

4 Now drag the point to file to the target file, while pressing the mouse button.

5 The link will automatically be inserted as text at the end of the document. This procedure makes sense only if you have no definite page elements to which you want to connect the link.

How to insert an absolute (external) link:

1 Select the text or the image.

2 Enter the full address. This must contain the protocol, the location, the domain and the top level domain, e.g. `http://www.intermedia.net/index.htm`

3 Confirm with ⏎.

Defining targets

After you have inserted the hyperlink, you can decide where the link should be opened, in the newly loaded destination document.

First of all, targets are used in frames. You will find more information about this in Chapter 7.

Nevertheless, there are two target definitions in the drop-down menu in the Property Inspector, which you can also set on "simple" Web pages:

- **target=«_blank«:** The linked documents are opened in a new, empty browser window. The previous document where the link was found remains open in the old browser window.

- **target=«_self«:** The link replaces the content in the current window with the new document.

How to set a target:

1 Insert a hyperlink as described in Chapter 5.

2 Make sure that the whole hyperlink is marked.

3 Set the target in the drop-down menu in the Property Inspector.

> **TIP**
>
> *Dreamweaver can update all relative links in a site in one file, which you have renamed. You set this option in the PREFERENCES (in the menu bar under EDIT) in the UPDATE LINKS WHEN MOVING FILES drop-down menu from the GENERAL category:*
>
>

Named anchors

A named anchor consists of two parts:

- A text marker **<a name></a>**, called the anchor, and
- the command, to get to this defined reference target.

> **TIP**
>
> *Subdivide long documents. The different parts can be jumped to directly from an index list. With labels, however, you can also allow the user to jump to the beginning of the document.*

How to create a named anchor:

1 First determine the place where the link should refer to later on. Open this document and select the corresponding place. Or simply place the cursor on the point you want to select.

2 Select INSERT/INVISIBLE TAGS/NAMED ANCHOR.

Or click on Ctrl + Alt + A. The INSERT NAMED ANCHOR dialog box appears:

3 Type in the name of the anchor. This should be a lower case word or a number.

4 Click on OK.

5 Then create a link to this named anchor: link to the document – as described before – where the anchor is placed. The result looks as follows:

First comes the name of the HTML file, then comes the hash #, and, finally, the named anchor.

6 When the anchors are put in the same document, you can enter these names directly in the HYPERLINK text box in the Property Inspector. No empty spaces are allowed between # and the name!

Alternatively, drag the point to file to the named anchor.

> **NOTE**
>
> *To be able to see the NAMED ANCHOR, you will need to set this in the Dreamweaver preferences. The VIEW/VISUAL AIDS/INVISIBLE TAGS needs to be activated.*

E-mail references

This is what a link to an e-mail address looks like in HTML:

`<a href="mailto:info@cybertechnics.co.uk">E-mail address</a>`

How to insert an e-mail reference:

1 Select the corresponding text or the linked image.

2 Select INSERT/EMAIL LINK from the menu bar of the document window or click on the ▣ button in the Object manager.

3 The highlighted text now appears in the INSERT EMAIL LINK window. You can change this afterwards.

4 Type in the e-mail address in the E-MAIL text box.

5 Click on OK to close the dialog window and to insert the link.

Checking links

Dreamweaver can check hyperlinks in a document

1 Select FILE/CHECK LINKS or press ⇧ + F8. All of the broken links will be listed in the LINK CHECKER window.

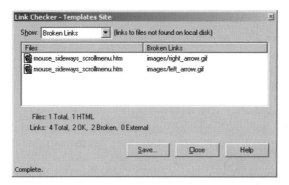

2 Click on the BROKEN LINKS entry to make another connection. You can also select the linked page using the browser icon now displayed, and then determine a new one in the Property Inspector. If the links occur frequently, Dreamweaver will ask if all the links that occur should be changed.

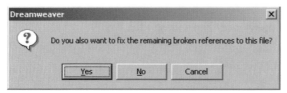

NOTE

In the SHOW drop-down menu of the link checker, you are able to determine very accurately what should be checked:

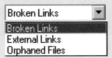

Orphaned files can only be checked if the whole site or a sub directory is checked.

TIPS

- *To check links in all the local sites, select SITE/CHECK LINKS SITEWIDE (Ctrl + F8). You can store the list of results as a TXT file.*

- *Dreamweaver shows you the external hyperlinks you should check. Enter these in the address box in your browser.*

- *You can change all the links on your site with a few clicks.*

How to change a link to a particular file for the whole site:

1 Select SITE/CHANGE LINKS SITEWIDE in the SITE WINDOW.

2 Enter the corresponding addresses (HTML, images, e-mail, etc.) or click on the folder icon and search through your computer for the desired file.

The original name of the link appears in the upper text box; the current reference to be used appears in the lower one.

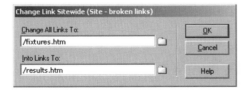

3 Click on OK. All files will then be listed in the UPDATE FILES dialog box.

4 Select either UPDATE or DON'T UPDATE.

Chapter 6

Tables

Tables (visible and invisible) are the basis of all page layouts. With this tool, you can position text and images not only horizontally but also vertically. This chapter shows how you can quickly and easily create and change tables in Dreamweaver.

All tables consist of:

- Rows (horizontal)
- Columns (vertical)
- Cells (smallest unit in a table placed in a specific row and column).

Standard and layout view

In Dreamweaver 4, there are two possible views: the standard view and the layout view.

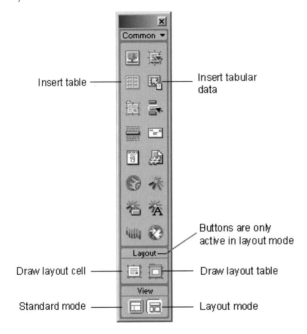

Insert table

Insert tabular data

Buttons are only active in layout mode

Draw layout cell

Draw layout table

Standard mode

Layout mode

With both icons in the Object manager you can switch between layout ⊟ and standard view ⊟. If you are in the layout mode, the 'Draw layout cell' and 'Draw layout table' buttons are active.

With ▣ you create a table (DRAW LAYOUT TABLE) and with ▣ single cells (DRAW LAYOUT CELL).

In the standard mode, click on the INSERT TABLES ⊞ button. You will find an adequate entry in the menu bar under INSERT/TABLE. Alternatively, press Ctrl + Alt + Del.

The standard view is particularly suitable for inserting contents in a table.

With the layout view, you could simply and quickly format cells, cut out, copy or move them.

You will learn, with practical examples, in the respective chapters, how to work with the individual modes.

Creating a table

Depending on which view you are in, the table will be created differently.

In the standard view, you insert a table in your document in the following way:

1 Click where you want to have the table inserted in your document.

2 Press the INSERT TABLE ⊞ button in the object panel.

Or, select INSERT/TABLE in the menu bar of the document window.

Alternatively, press Ctrl + Alt + Del .

3 The INSERT TABLE dialog box appears.

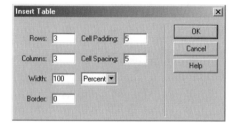

4 Enter the number of rows and columns, the table size, the borders as well as cell padding and cell spacing (see page 168) of the table. In doing so, you have determined the basic structure of the table. Later on, you will read about how to change this.

5 Click on OK to insert the table.

That was the traditional method. Now, let us take a look at the new tools Dreamweaver 4 offers for inserting a table. You must make a decision about how you would like to work. The result is the same in any case.

In the layout view you insert a table in the following way:

1 Press the 🔲 button (DRAW LAYOUT TABLE) in the Object manager. The mouse pointer now becomes a cross.

2 You will see the outline of the table in the document window.

Alternatively, use the 🔲 tool (DRAW LAYOUT CELL). Dreamweaver automatically creates the table for you.

3 Click on the DRAW LAYOUT CELL button in the Object manager if you wish to insert cells in the table. The cross appears here as well, with the outline of the cell spread out.

To create a layout for an independent table, you also have the option of clicking in the document window where the lower, right hand corner of the table is to be based. By doing so, the table always begins at the left edge of the document. You cannot create nested tables (see below) in this way.

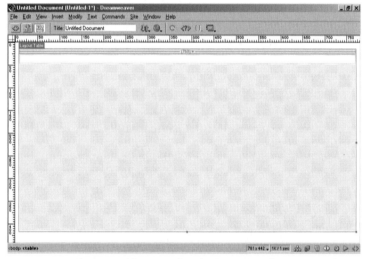

Figure 6.1: *This is a table created in the layout mode. You can change the size afterwards by dragging one of the three "handles". If you click on the arrow beside the table size, you can determine the table properties (see Editing tables on page 159)*

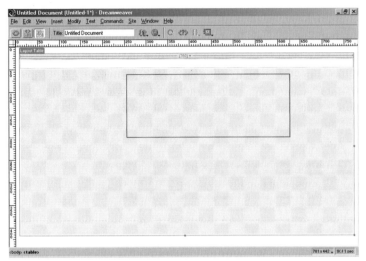

Figure 6.2: Press the DRAW LAYOUT CELL button. And pull the single cells in the table. In this example, the second cell is created. Change the cell size by pulling the "handle" (see Chapter 6)

Creating nested tables:

WHAT IS THIS?

Nested tables *are tables within tables. This means that you can insert as many tables as you like in a cell. The inserted tables can then contain additional tables.*

1 In the cell, click where you want to insert an additional table.

2 In the STANDARD VIEW, insert a table as described above (steps 2 to 4).

3 If you work in the LAYOUT MODE, follow steps 1 to 3 above.

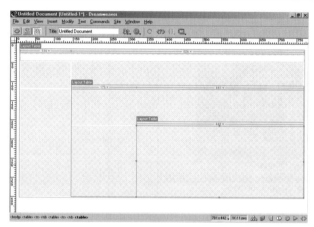

Figure 6.3: Move a new table into a table cell. Here you can see three tables nested inside each other

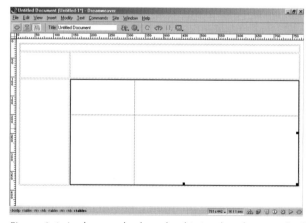

Figure 6.4: In the standard mode, this is what the page looks like

Adding content

You can insert text, images or other objects in a table. If you would like to insert content in an empty table cell, you must be in the standard mode.

157

Inserting text and images:

1 Click in the cell where you want to insert contents.

2 Type in the text or insert this in the intermediate file (see Chapter 3). Place images (see Chapter 4) or other elements in the corresponding cell.

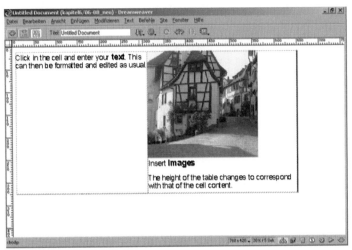

The cell height automatically adapts to the content of the cell (see Width and height on page 160).

> **TIP**
>
> *Press the* [⇆] *key to skip to the next cell. Press* [⇧] + [⇆] *to get to the previous cell. You can also use the arrow key for this.*

Importing existing table data:

You can insert data from applications other than Dreamweaver (such as Excel) and then continue to edit this. However, the data items must be separated from each other by commas, tabs, semicolons or other signs. A TXT file, for example, fulfils this requirement.

1 Select FILE/IMPORT/IMPORT TABLE DATA. The IMPORT TABLE DATA dialog window appears.

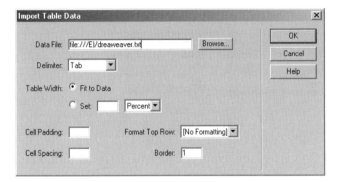

2 Enter the directory and the name of the file you want to insert in the DATA FILE box. Use the BROWSE button to search for the file on your computer.

3 Set the DELIMITER, used in the document to be imported.

4 Carry out any possible additional formatting, such as setting cell padding and cell spacing.

> CAUTION
>
> *If you do not set any DELIMITERS, the data may not be imported correctly. However, you will not be given any warning message about this, so be careful.*

Editing tables

The display in the Property Inspector will change depending on what you have selected.

When a table is highlighted, it may look as follows:

When a cell is highlighted, it looks like this:

159

Use the Property Inspector to add or change properties of tables and cells.

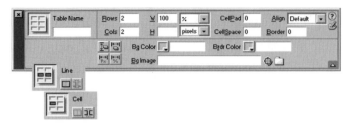

In the APPLY button, you can see which part of the table you have selected. The name of the highlighted object stands beside this. You can edit this using the Property Inspector.

Width and height

There are various options for working on a table afterwards. On one hand, you can change between standard and layout mode, and on the other, there are different possibilities.

TIP

*Activate grid and rulers using **View** in the menu bar.*

How to determine the size of a table in the standard mode:

1 Highlight the table by right clicking on the table and then click on the command TABLE/SELECT TABLE from the context menu that appears.

You will also find this command under MODIFY in the menu bar. The shortcut is Ctrl + A.

Or, click on the table border in the document window.

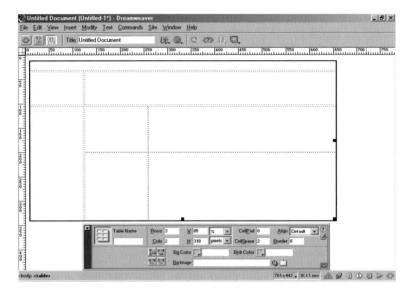

2 Enter new values for the width in the Property Inspector. They can be in fixed pixel size (absolute value) or in percentage values (relative). Determine this in the drop-down menu:

In order to create a layout, you don't necessarily need to enter a value in the cell height. This automatically adapts to the cell padding.

3 Confirm with ⏎ or click on the APPLY button.

> **NOTE**
>
> • *Depending on what kind of content you insert, you may need to change the fixed pixel width in a table. For example, when an image is too large or a long word cannot be broken down.*
>
> • *The same applies for the cell height. If you have not determined a height, this will adapt to the cell padding.*

The Property Inspector is equipped with buttons with which you can quickly change the size of a table.

Use the buttons above to delete dimensional information. With the two bottom ones, you give a relative instruction from a fixed table width, and, in reverse, a fixed size from a relative table. Pay attention to the measurements of your Dreamweaver window.

> **TIP**
>
> *You can edit, copy, cut out, move or delete a marked table.*

How to determine the width and the height of a table in the layout mode:

1 Mark the table by clicking either on the green frame or on the LAYOUT TABLE index.

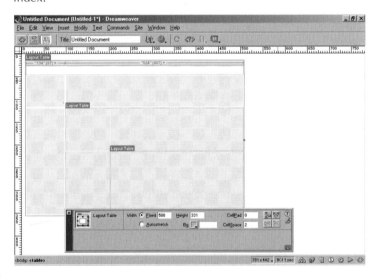

2 Pull the right handle to alter the table width, pull the bottom one to alter the height and, to alter the width and height proportionally, pull the handle in the corner.

Or, insert the corresponding value in the Property Inspector.

> **NOTE**
>
> *By scaling a table in the layout mode, the size of the interpreted cells will remain unchanged. Instead, Dreamweaver inserts a new row or column. A cell without dimensional information will be assigned a pixel value.*

In layout mode you will always be able to clear dimensional information (see below). You will also find the buttons for this in the Property Inspector:

Scaling cells, rows and columns (standard mode):

1 Move the mouse over the border lines of the cell, line or column whose size you want to change. The mouse pointer changes to a double arrow.

2 With a held down mouse button, move the border line to the new position.

Here, the first cell will be smaller, the second becomes larger.

Or:

Highlight the row or column you would like to alter, by moving over the cells with a depressed mouse button.

Place the mouse at the beginning of a row or a column. An arrow appears. Now click. The corresponding row or column is now selected.

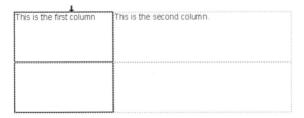

3 Alternatively, enter the new value in the corresponding text box in the Property Inspector.

4 Press ⏎ or click on the APPLY button.

> NOTE
>
> To **align a table,** mark it and then select the desired option in the drop-down menu in the Property Inspector: left, centre or right.
>
>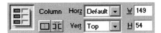
>
> By default, your table will be aligned with the left edge if you don't give an instruction.

How to determine the width of a cell in layout mode:

1 Cells that you can work on glow up when you move the mouse over them. By default, Dreamweaver will display such a cell in red (you will be instructed how to alter this setting below).

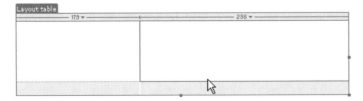

2 Click on a cell. It now appears in blue (also a changeable default setting). In addition, eight handles become visible.

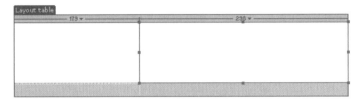

3 Pull the handles until you get the size you want.

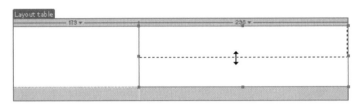

> **CAUTION**
>
> *In the layout mode, you cannot alter whole rows or columns.*

How to determine the maximum width of a column in the layout mode:

In the layout mode, you define the column width in the individual cells. You can assign a relative width or a fixed size to two equally large cells, if they are placed on top of each other.

- Select MAKE COLUMN AUTOSTRETCH from the drop-down menu in the table layout:

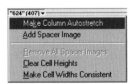

The fixed column width will then be replaced by a relative value (100%). This means that the other cells will be minimised as far as possible, and the relative column will be set to the maximum size – with respect to the defined table size.

In the layout view, you can see this setting on the ▭〜▾▭ symbol.

165

This is how you can scale a table with the aid of invisible images:

1 Select ADD SPACER IMAGE in the drop-down menu.

2 When you call this function for the first time, Dreamweaver will ask if you would like to create a spacer image or if you would like to use an existing spacer image file.

The location where these images are saved is now left in PREFERENCES (LAYOUT VIEW). If you would like to define a new image as a **spacer image**, you will need to change the entry here.

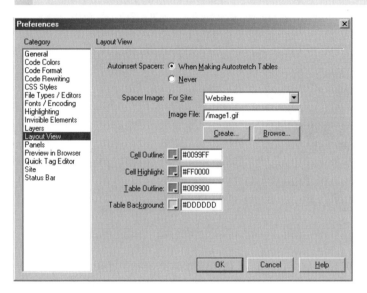

3 Determine where to save the spacer image in the dialog window now opened, or select an existing spacer image.

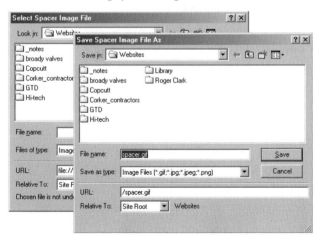

The spacer image will be inserted in a new row at the end of the table. In this way, it is in the same column. The row and the image will be about 1 pixel high.

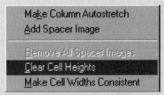
Merging cells

When you have created your table in **layout mode**, your table will possibly already contain merged cells – depending on how you have arranged your cells.

- If you would like to change this setting, simply grab the cells from the handle and move these to the desired position.

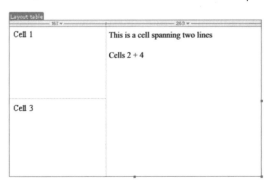

In this example, the second column spreads over two lines and thereby merges cell 2 with cell 4.

In the **standard view** it is somewhat different:

1 Select the cell you would like to merge.

Cell 1	Cell 2
Cell 3	Cell 4

2 Click on the MERGE SELECTED CELLS USING SPANS ⊞ button in the Property Inspector.

The marked cells 2 and 4 are now merged:

Cell 1	Cell 2
Cell 3	Cell 4

> **TIP**
>
> *When you would like to split merged cells into single cells, select them and in the Property Inspector click on the SPLIT CELL INTO ROWS OR COLUMNS button ⊞ .*

Splitting cells

To split merged cells:

1 Click on the ⊞ button in the Property Inspector.

2 From the dialog window, select how you would like to merge the cells.

169

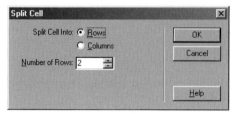

Determine the number of rows or columns.

3 Confirm with OK.

4 The cell is now split again.

> **NOTE**
>
> *Make sure that the content of the cell you are splitting is placed in the first cell (meaning in the upper left cell).*

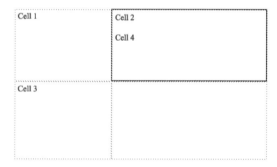

Cell padding and cell spacing

> **WHAT IS THIS?**
>
> ***Cell padding*** *defines the number of pixels between the contents of a cell and the cell borders. The HTML command is called* `cellpadding`.
>
> ***Cell spacing*** *defines the number of pixels between the individual cells. It is defined as* `cellspacing` *in the source code.*

For an existing table, define the cell padding and cell spacing in the following way:

1 Select the table.

2 Type in the (pixel) value in the corresponding text box in the Property Inspector.

3 Confirm with the ⏎ key or click on the APPLY button.

> **TIP**
>
> *When you are defining a table in the standard mode, you can enter the pixel values for cell padding and cell spacing.*

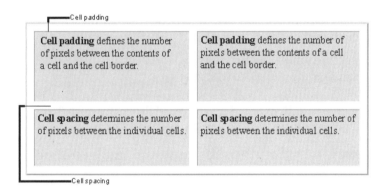

Figure 6.5:   Here, you can see the difference between cell padding and cell spacing. Cell padding and cell spacing are 10 pixels respectively. To see the inside of a cell better, the table is coloured (see Colours and background on page 173). In addition, the border width is defined to 2 pixels

Borders

1 Select the table.

2 Enter the desired border width in the BORDER text box in the Property Inspector.

If you would like to lay out the page with a table, define an invisible table
with the border width of 0.

If the table should not be visible in Dreamweaver, you can change this in the
menu bar under VIEW/VISUAL AIDS/TABLE BORDERS.

3 To give the border a colour, simply click on the colour palette, which is found in
the Property Inspector.

Brdr Color [ ] #FF0000

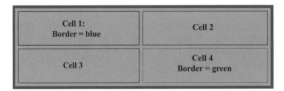

You can determine a border colour for the whole table. If there are other
defined border colours, these will be displayed.

Cell 1: Border = blue	Cell 2
Cell 3	Cell 4 Border = green

Colours and background

1 Select the cells or the whole table; everything that you want to colour.

2 In the Property Inspector, click on the PAINTBOX.

In the following example, the background image displaces the table colour. The cell colour covers the background image.

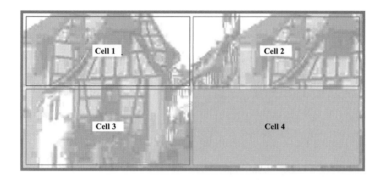

TIP

You will find the design templates for the tables under COMMANDS/ FORMAT TABLE.

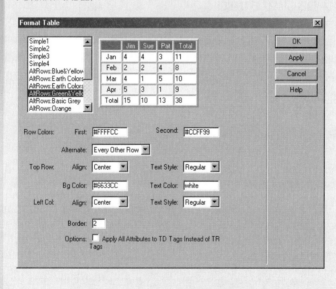

TIP

Select rows, columns or cells and format the text in one go (see Chapter 3).

Aligning cell padding

The content of a cell could be aligned horizontally just like a paragraph. It is also possible to have vertical alignment.

1 Select the cells that should have the content aligned either vertically or horizontally.

2 Select left, centred or right from the drop-down menu for the horizontal alignment.

You can also use the corresponding buttons for the paragraph alignment:

3 To align the content of a vertical cell, you need to click on the corresponding drop-down menu.

Defining a header line

In the header line, you can give the table a title and give a description of the content. Browsers represent the header line differently. Text in this line will usually be displayed centred and in bold.

> **TIP**
>
> *Format the content of a cell by selecting this and indicating the font, font size and other types of text formatting in the Property Inspector (see Chapter 3).*

1 Go into the standard mode.

2 Click on the cell (usually the first cell) which you would like to define as header line.

3 Activate the HEADER check box in the Property Inspector.

Header ☑

The header line appears detached from the other table contents.

Date	Place	Event
3rd-6th	Bridlington	Carnival
3rd-6th	Scarborough	Carnival
3rd-6th	Whitby	Carnival
3rd-6th	Rotherham	Fete
3rd-6th	Barnsley	Beer festival
3rd-6th	Sheffield	Beer festival
3rd-6th	Leeds	Beer festival
3rd-6th	Doncaster	Film festival
3rd-6th	Huddersfield	Carnival
3rd-6th	Halifax	Fete
3rd-6th	Wakefield	Fete
3rd-6th	Dewsbury	Fete

NOTE

You can define both a line, a column and the contents of a single cell as header line.

No wrapping

Usually, the text will be wrapped and therefore adjusted to the cell width. You can turn this off with the NO WRAP option.

1 Highlight the cell, column or row where you do not want any wrapping to occur.

2 Activate the NO WRAP check box in the Property Inspector.

This cell adjusts to the text because the wrap has been deactivated.	This text is broken up.

CAUTION

If the NO WRAP function is activated, the cells may become enlarged to fit the text in.

Adding cells

1 Select the table. You are now able to read the number of cells and rows in the Property Inspector.

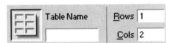

2 To alter the number of cells, enter new values in the ROWS text box.

If you would like to change the number of columns, type in the number in the COLS text box.

3 Press the ⏎ key or click on the Apply button.

The rows will be inserted below the table, columns to the right.

When you wish to insert a row in a specific position in the existing table:

1 Click above where you would like to insert the cell.

2 Select MODIFY/TABLE/INSERT ROW or press Ctrl + M.

To insert a column in a particular position:

1 Click on the column to the left of where you wish to insert a column.

2 Select MODIFY/TABLE/INSERT COLUMN or press Ctrl + ⇧ + A.

How to insert several cells or columns:

1 Click on the cell next to where you would like to insert a row or column. Or select the whole column or row.

2 Select MODIFY/TABLE/INSERT ROWS OR COLUMNS.

3 Establish what you would like to insert in the INSERT ROWS OR COLUMNS dialog window and indicate the number. You then decide whether the row(s) or column(s) should be inserted above or below the current cursor position or selection.

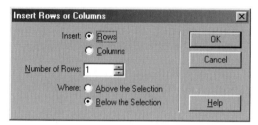

4 Click on OK.

TIP

Right click on the table to open the context menu. Here you will find all the commands described on the menu bar.

Deleting cells

1 Click on a cell in the row or column that you want to delete.

2 To delete a row, select MODIFY/TABLE/DELETE ROW or TABLE/DELETE ROW from the context menu.

And what happens in the source code?

A table is defined by three tags:

- With <table> you tell the browser that a table is starting.

- <tr> defines the first row.

- There must be at least one cell in the row (otherwise it would not be a row). The <td> is used for this.

The following table is a 2x2 table. This means that both rows consist of two cells.

Cell 1 = red	Cell 2 = blue
Cell 4	Cell 5

The table has a yellow background. The first cell is coloured red, the second is blue. The two bottom ones have no colour. You can see the table background here.

The HTML code looks like this:

```
<TABLE BORDER="1" WIDTH="75%" BGCOLOR="#FFCC00">

 <TR BGCOLOR="#33FF66">

  <TD bgcolor="#FF0000" width="33%">cell 1 = red</TD>

  <TD BGCOLOR="#7B7BD2" width="33%">cell 2 = blue</TD>

 </TR>

 <TR>

  <TD width="33%">cell 4</TD>

  <TD width="33%">cell 5</TD>

 </TR>

</TABLE>
```

179

Chapter 7

Frames

Frames are best suited for keeping a navigation bar or an index directory or a tool bar permanently visible – independent of whether the user scrolls down the whole page and what Web page is opened on the Web site. Using buttons, you can go directly from one document to another.

Using frames, you are also able to create clever layouts. In this chapter, we will learn to build a new frameset. You will learn how to edit and alter frames. We will create a navigation bar with which you can open documents in other frames.

Frames consist of two parts: a frameset and a content document, the actual frame.

The **frameset** is an HTML page which defines the structure of the visible documents (frames) to each other. A frame is also a single HTML document. It is defined in the frameset which documents should be displayed, where these are to be put and in what size. The frameset moves into the background as a kind of control element and holds the documents together.

The frameset is also described as the "superior frame" and a frame as a "subordinate frame".

In Dreamweaver, you can create the frameset and integrate new or existing pages as frames at the same time, editing the content and linking them.

The frameset in the following example consists of four frames. Every frame is an independent document.

You will see the structure of the frameset in the Frame Inspector.

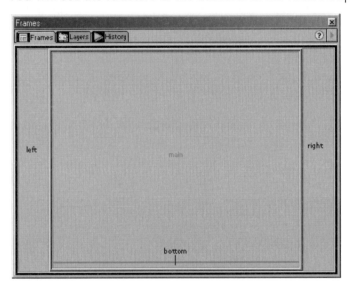

Creating framesets

You can design the frameset yourself, or select one of the various design templates in Dreamweaver. You can use both methods in your work. In the Changing the layout section on page 194, you will learn how you can edit these framesets further and assign specific properties for the whole frameset or for the individual frames.

> **NOTE**
>
> *Work in the design window. Frames can also be created in the standard view and in the layout view.*

Frameset templates

The structure is defined in predefined framesets. A predefined standard size is assigned to the frames. In addition, every frame has a name.

1 Open an HTML page that will be a component of a frameset, or work on a new, empty file.

2 Click on the document in the design window.

3 Open the FRAMES panel in the Object manager.

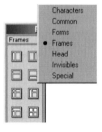

4 Select a frameset template by clicking on the corresponding button.

Pay attention to the blue marking in the button: this symbolises the content frame. The white area stands for the new frames.

WHAT IS THIS?

Content frame *is the content of a Web page. Depending on which button is pressed in the navigation bar (or on other pages), a new document will be loaded here.*

Or press the button in the document (important in nested frames; see below).

Alternatively, select the desired template from INSERT/FRAME from the menu bar.

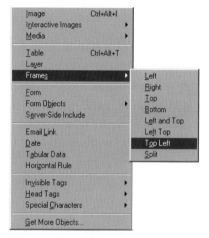

 If you split a document into frames, you create separate HTML documents for the frameset and for every new frame. An open document is now in the content frame of your frameset.

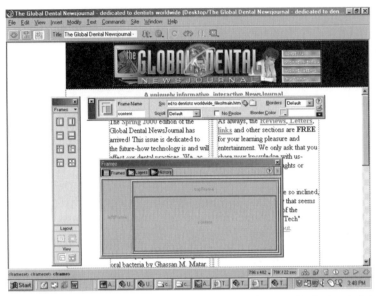

In this classical structure, the navigation bar, which is visible on all the pages, is placed on the left. Usually, it doesn't change its appearance. With the buttons in this bar, you are able to change the content of the right content frame.

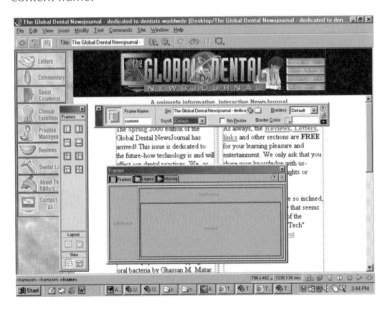

This frameset can also be laid out with empty documents. Therefore, the first icon in the Object manager will be used here. Both frames have a predefined width and a name assigned to them. This is easily recognised in the Frame Inspector.

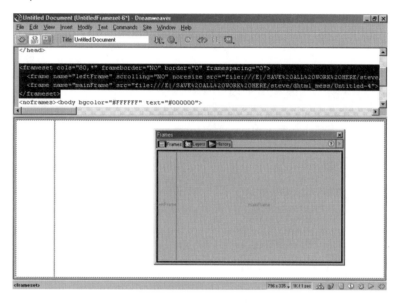

TIP

You can also continue to work on the predefined frameset (see the Changing the layout section on page 194).

You will learn how to develop these framesets further in the sections Creating a frameset without a template (page 188) and Nested framesets (page 191). You can skip the rest of the Creating framesets section if you are happy with the basic structure.

NOTE

To change the width of a frame, you simply move the frame to the desired position.

Creating a frameset without a template

The basic structure of a frame frameset can be altered individually. In addition, there are other ways to create a frameset.

How to make your own frameset:

1 Open an empty window or an existing HTML document.

2 Select MODIFY/FRAMESET from the menu bar.

Your document is subdivided into two equally large parts. The frames have not yet been assigned any names.

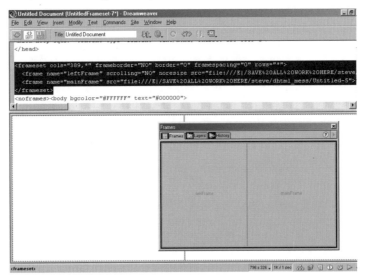

> **NOTE**
>
> *In this example, you work with **one** frameset. You can easily see this in the HTML source code. The **<Frameset>** tag encloses all the frames.*
>
> *You can also establish several (nested) framesets in an HTML page (see Changing the layout on page 194).*

If you have opened an existing document, this document will become a component of the frameset (see Frameset templates on page 184). Depending on the option selected, this content will be displayed in the corresponding place.

By doing this, you have set the bottom grid of your site. You can then manually drag further frames into the document window.

3 To add further frames (or to divide a frame), pull the outer, vertical or horizontal frame in the document window.

> **TIP**
>
> *Activate VIEW/VISUAL AIDS/FRAME BORDERS in the menu bar. The borders that surround the document now appear wider. Follow the method described above (3). The window is split.*

If you would like to split the document into four frames, pull the borders from one of the corners in the document window.

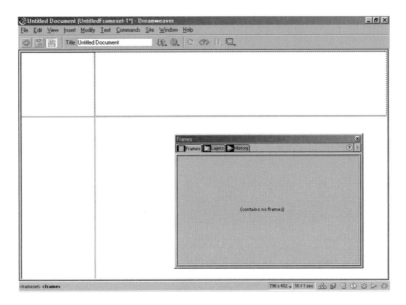

If you would like to split up a frame even further (either horizontally or vertically), pull one of the inner borders to the appropriate place.

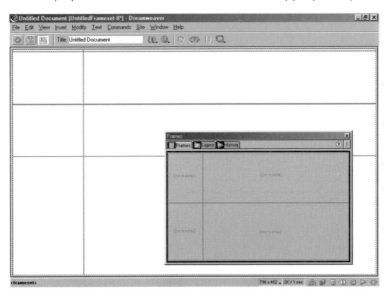

> **CAUTION**
>
> *Think of every frameset or frame as an individual file. You will have to save all the frameset files and all documents loaded in the frames (see Margins on page 201).*

Nested framesets

> **WHAT IS THIS?**
>
> *A **nested frameset** is a frameset within another frameset. This means that you can insert framesets inside each other just as you like. Again, all of them consist of the frameset file and the single frame documents. Several **<frameset>** tags are saved in the HTML source code.*

1 Click in the frame into which you would like to insert another frameset.

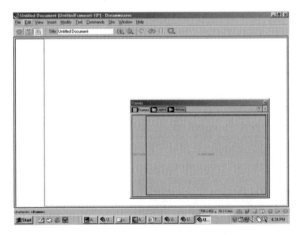

2 Select MODIFY/FRAMESET and one of the listed options.

Or, press on a frameset button in the FRAMES panel in the Object window.

Or select the desired template from INSERT/FRAME in the menu bar.

The document is split up according to your instructions.

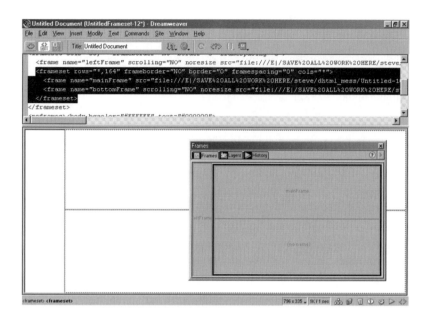

You will recognise from the HTML source code that there are two framesets saved here. The right content frame of the first frameset contains another frameset, which consists of two horizontal frames. The second frameset is selected. This is seen on the dotted line in the design window and on the display in the Frame Inspector.

Selecting frames or framesets

You can select individual frames or framesets using the Frame Inspector.

The Frame Inspector shows you the structure of the calculated frameset very clearly, and thus makes the choice of documents much easier.

How to open the Frame Inspector:

* Select WINDOW/FRAMES from the menu bar or press ⇧ + F2.

  Framesets are indicated by a thick, three-dimensional frame.

  Frames are marked with thin, grey lines. And the name is displayed in every frame.

How to select the frame:

* Click on the frame in the Frame Inspector.

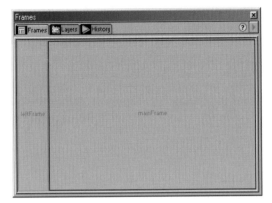

In this example, the right frame was selected.

How to select a frameset:

* In the Frame Inspector, click on the frame surrounding the other frames.

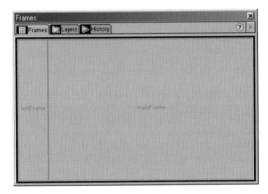

NOTE

You can also select framesets and frames in the document window. To do this, click on the frame border. To select a single frame, click on the frame with a depressed Alt *key (Windows) or* Alt-⇧ *(Macintosh). A dotted selection line appears.*

If you have selected a frameset or a frame, you can define the properties with the Property Inspector (see Altering the width and height of a frame below).

Changing the layout

There is an infinite number of options for laying out frames. In the previous section you saw how to create the basic frameset by either splitting existing frames or laying out new framesets.

Deleting frames

You can continue to split the frames until you have achieved the desired layout. Nevertheless, if one frame too many has been created, you can quite easily get rid of it:

1 While pressing the mouse button, drag the frame border off the page or to the border of primary frames.

2 Release the mouse button. The frame is deleted.

> **TIP**
>
> *Before you delete a frame, you have the option of inserting the content of this frame into another:*
>
> *1. Select the element you would like to move.*
>
> *2. Move this to another frame while pressing the mouse button.*
>
> *3. Release the mouse button. The object is now moved.*

Altering the width and height of a frame

As with tables, framesets are split into rows and columns. These frames have a specific height and width.

1 Pull the frame border to the desired position while pressing the mouse button. The mouse pointer changes to a double arrow.

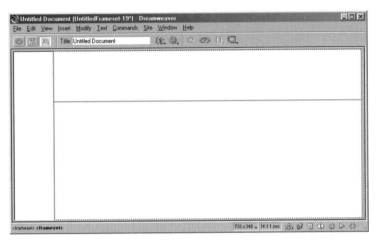

2 Release the mouse button.

There are other parallels with tables (see Chapter 6). You can always determine the width of frames with a pixel value. Alternatively, you can define relative instructions.

> **TIP**
>
> *Define the width and the height for a column and a row in pixels and give all the other measurements relative to this area.*

An example:

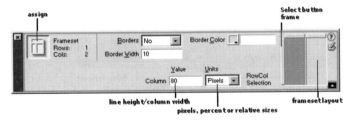

The left frame has an 80 pixel width. Its height is relatively defined. The width of the upper frame is relative, but the height is absolute (80 pixels). All the sizes of the third frame are defined relative to this.

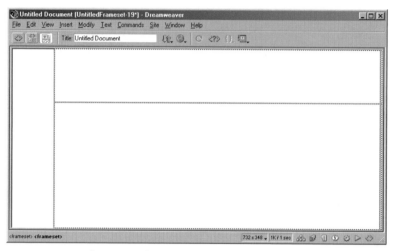

Here you see the same frameset in a larger window. More clearly: the left frame has a fixed width (80 pixels). The upper frame has not changed as well. The content frame, on the other hand, has altered its size relatively.

Use the Property Inspector to determine the width of a frame in pixels:

1 Select the frameset.

2 Highlight the frame whose size you would like to determine. Click for this on the FRAMESET LAYOUT in the Property Inspector or select the SELECT FRAME button which is beside this.

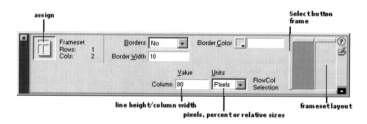

Click on the expanding arrow if all of the details are not displayed.

3 Type in a value in the Row text box.

4 Select the units:

- **Pixel** determines a precise width and height.

- **Percent** refers to the frameset size.

- **Relative** means that the width or height adapts to the remaining space. This frame fills the rest of the available room.

5 To apply the modifications to the frameset, click on the APPLY button.

6 Repeat these steps for the other frames.

Inserting content

Now you can insert content into the frameset you have created. You can either insert new content or connect existing pages. Since every page is an individual document, they all have a specific URL assigned.

Integrating an existing page

To connect a frame to an existing page, proceed as follows:

1 Highlight the frame where you want to insert the content. The properties are displayed in the Property Inspector.

2 In the directory, type in the name of the document in the SOURCE text box.

Or, click on the BROWSE button to select a specific file on your hard drive.

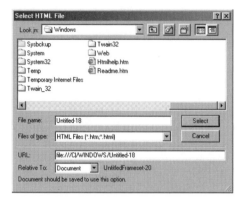

3 Select the corresponding file you want to load in the frame, then click on the SELECT button.

Or, drag the POINT TO FILE ⊕ to the corresponding file in the site window (see Chapter 5).

> **TIP**
>
> *In the Property Inspector, determine which document should be displayed in which frame. In addition, you can carry out further adjustments — especially border qualities.*

Defining new content

You can work in the individual frames as normal if you have opened a frameset. You can integrate all of the elements that you can implement in a "normal" page.

Frameset options

Borders

1 Highlight the frameset.

2 Select one of the following options from BORDERS in the Property Inspector:

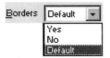

Yes: The border is displayed.

No: No frames are displayed.

Standard: Uses the default setting of the browser (normally means YES).

3 If you would like to determine the BORDER WIDTH, you enter the value in the text box Border Width [   ] .

4 To determine the border colour, you use the colour palette or enter the hexadecimal code directly (see Chapter 2 and Page properties, Background):

Border Color ▣ #CC0000

5 Click on the APPLY button or press [↵].

TIP

The standard frame width is 5 pixels. You can change this in the Property Inspector.

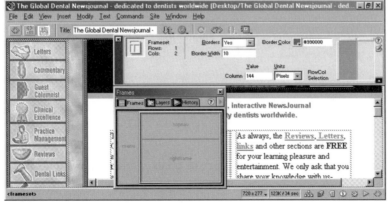

A border of 10 pixels is defined between the two frames. The display of the border is selected from the drop-down menu. The border is red.

The same frameset with a border width of 0 looks like this:

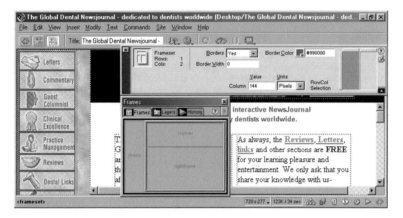

Margins

1 Highlight the frame whose margins you would like to determine.

2 Enter pixel values for the margin width and the margin height in the corresponding text boxes in the Property Inspector.

3 Assign these qualities to the frame by clicking on the APPLY button or pressing the ↵ button.

An example: the individual frames have been assigned different values for the margins.

Marginwidth=0 Marginheight=0	Marginwidth=10 Marginheight=10
Marginwidth=20 Marginheight=20	Marginwidth=30 Marginheight=30

CAUTION

Netscape interprets the margin settings of the frames as well as the page properties. The margins defined here are more important. By doing this, the frame margins are ignored.

In Internet Explorer, the opposite happens: the page properties are ignored if the margins are defined in the frames.

Scrollbars

WHAT IS THIS?

*You move the page (meaning the content of a frame) from top to bottom using a **vertical scrollbar**. The **horizontal scrollbar** moves the document from right to left.*

1 Highlight the frame to which you want to assign a scrollbar.

2 Select one of the following options from the SCROLL drop-down menu in the Property Inspector:

201

Yes: The scrollbar is always visible.

No: The scrollbar is not visible.

Auto: The scrollbar is only displayed when it is necessary, that is, when the document is too large for the frame.

Default: Uses the default setting of the browser (usually corresponds to AUTO).

These settings relate to both the horizontal and vertical scrollbars.

An example: in this Web page, you can only scroll in the right content frame. A scrollbar is inserted if the document is higher or wider than the window. In the source code, the AUTO option controls this. The scrollbar is turned off in the menu bar.

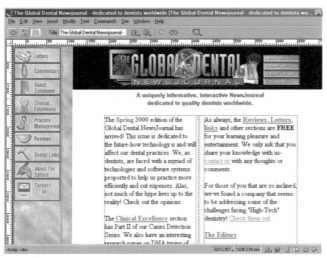

In the following illustration you will see clearly how to control the indication of the scrollbar with the different options.

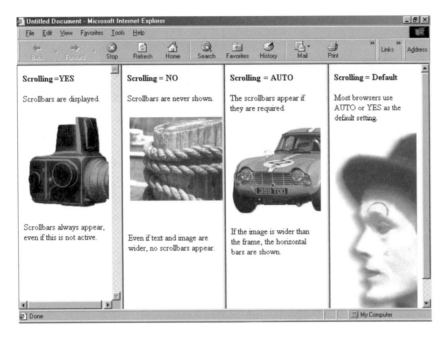

No resize

If the user is not in the position to alter the size of specific frames, the NO RESIZE ☐ No Resize must be activated. First, highlight the corresponding frame.

This will mean that the size of the neighbouring frames cannot be changed.

Controlling the frame content with hyperlinks

Clicking on a hyperlink in a simple document will load up the called HTML page in the same browser and will replace the previous document (see Chapter 5).

You probably would not like to have this effect in a frame. The navigation bar, for example, should remain visible on all pages. The solution to this is simple: tell the link where it should load the page.

We pick up the example from The Global Dental News Journal again:

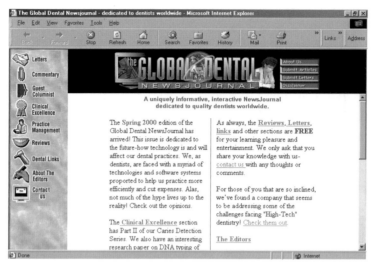

Here you see a static navigation bar appearing on all of the pages. The right content frame will adapt its contents according to the button you have selected or to the activated hyperlink.

The next thing you need to do is name the different frames. In addition to this, you can define hyperlinks that open documents in other frames.

> NOTE
>
> *If you don't define a target, the new document will be loaded in the same frame.*

Naming frames

The browser only knows where to load the new document when the frame has a clear name. This is important if you would like to load the target document in another frame.

1 Highlight the frame in the Frame Inspector.

2 Enter the description in the FRAME NAME text box in the Property Inspector.

3 Confirm with ⏎ or click on the APPLY button.

> **TIPS**
>
> - *Use lower case letters and numbers. Blank spaces are not allowed.*
>
> - *If you have worked with the predefined framesets, the single frames already have names assigned to them.*
>
> - *If you lay out nested pages with predefined framesets, Dreamweaver uses the predefined names. Double naming is avoided since a number follows the name automatically.*
>
> - *Make sure that you have given clear identification in complex framesets. You can then find your way more easily.*
>
> - *Give the basic target in the <head> area: type in the target <base target="Frame name"> in the HTML editor.*

Defining targets

Documents can be loaded in the same frame in which they were placed in the hyperlink. Another option is to display the document in another frame. Navigation bars are frequently installed after the last variant which is visible (see Global Dental News Journal).

1 Highlight the text area or the image you wish to link.

2 Select the target document.

3 Type in the name of the target frame in the TARGET text field.

Alternatively, select the frame name (see Naming frames on page 204) from the same drop-down menu.

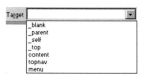

You do not need to provide the name of the frame, as you can define the default or basic target, which every browser can interpret (see below).

We have two general target entries in Chapter 5. When using Frames, this means:

- **target="_blank":** The linked document is opened in a new, empty browser window. The frame and the frameset, from which this link was called, remain open in the old browser window.

- **target="_self":** The linked document is opened in the same frame as where it was called from.

In addition, you can use two more target definitions in the frames:

- **target="_parent":** The link replaces the content in the current frame with the new document. The document is opened in the main window in encapsulated frames.

- **target="_top":** The link will be loaded in the whole browser window. All frames are replaced.

Save

Since a frameset consists of different documents, you will need to save these separately. If you have integrated a predefined document in a frameset, in order not to edit this any further you will only have to save the frameset.

How to save a frameset:

1 Highlight the frameset in the Frame Inspector.

2 Select FILE/SAVE FRAMESET AS or press [Ctrl] + [⇧] + [S]. The SAVE AS dialog window appears.

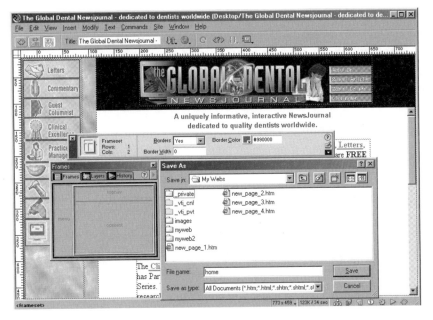

3 Determine the name of the file and the directory where you want to save your file.

4 Click on the SAVE button. The frameset is now saved.

How to save an individual frame:

1 Highlight the frame that you want to save in the Frame Inspector.

2 Select FILE/SAVE ALL FRAMES from the menu bar. The SAVE AS dialog window will appear.

3 Name the directory and the filename for the individual document and click on SAVE. The frames are now saved.

No frames

If a user who has a browser that cannot display frames visits your Web page, he/she will see nothing at all. Therefore, you should offer a **<noframe>** version.

How to create a <noframe> page:

1 Select MODIFY/FRAMESET/EDIT NOFRAMES CONTENT. The empty **<noframe>**-page will be displayed.

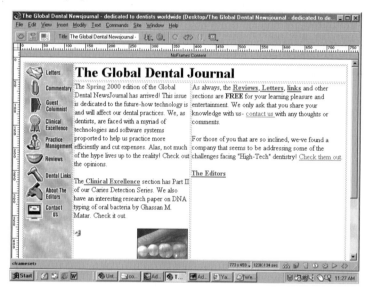

2 Edit this page as a normal HTML document: enter text, images, links, page properties, etc. You can also copy the content of an existing page.

3 To return to frame view, select MODIFY/FRAMESET/EDIT NO FRAMES CONTENT. The tick behind the NO FRAME view command is removed again.

And what happens in the source code?

> **NOTE**
>
> The **<frameset>** tag encapsulates all of the frames.
>
> In the **<frame>** tag, the name and the saving path of the document are anchored. This shall be displayed when the framesets are first opened. In addition to this, it contains information about the appearance and the actions of the individual frames.

Example:

```html
<html>
<head>
<title>The Global Dental News Journal</title>
</head>
<frameset framespacing="0" border="0" cols="144,*"
frameborder="YES">
<frame name="menu" target="content" src="target/menu.htm"
marginwidth="0" marginheight="0" scrolling="no" noresize>
<frame name="top" src="target/index.htm" marginwidth="0"
marginheight="0" scrolling="auto">
<noframes>
<body topmargin="0" leftmargin="0" background="images/menu/
back.gif" >
<p>Commentary</p>
<p>
<a href="letters/index.htm" target="_top">Here you find let-
ters to the editor. </a>
<img src="image.jpg" align="right">
</p>
</body>
</noframes>
</frameset>
</html>
```

Chapter 8

Forms

Using forms, visitors can give feedback on your site, submit orders to the online shop, apply to participate in events or simply ask a question. Make your Web site interactive. In this chapter, you will learn how to create a form and which form elements there are.

Creating a form

A form could be integrated into an existing Web site or inserted into an empty HTML document.

1 Click where the form should start in the document.

2 Select the INSERT/FORM command in the menu bar.

Or, open the Object manager under WINDOW/OBJECTS or Ctrl + F2.

Select the FORM panel. All the form elements are listed here (see Form elements on page 213).

3 Click on the INSERT FORM ▣ button.

The form is inserted into the document.

The red line marks the form in the design window. Elements are now inserted here. If you cannot see this line, select the check box FORM DELIMITER in the INVISIBLE ELEMENTS panel in the PREFERENCES dialog box (EDIT/PREFERENCES). Also check if the invisible elements are activated under VIEW/VISUAL AIDS.

The start and end `<form>` tags are inserted in the HTML source code.

4 In addition, you can determine the form properties. There is more information about this in this chapter.

> **NOTE**
>
> *By default, Dreamweaver puts a form over the whole width of the document window. With the help of tables, you can limit this size. In addition, you can structure your form with it.*

Form elements

How to insert elements in forms:

1 Click where you want to insert an element within the red form frame.

2 Click on the button of the element you wish to insert in the Object manager.

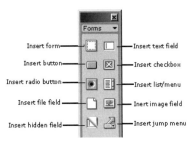

Or, select the corresponding object from INSERT/FORM OBJECTS in the menu bar.

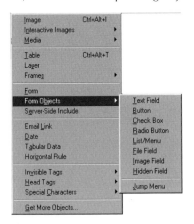

NOTE

A form can contain any HTML element (such as text, images, paragraphs, tables). However, you cannot insert a form into another form. Also, two or more individual forms on a single page are not permitted.

In the following form, a table has been inserted. In this table, all the possible form elements have been listed. The sequence is taken from the Object manager (from left to right and from top to bottom).

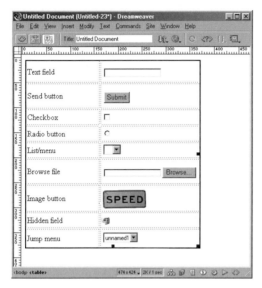

This is what a form may look like on the Web:

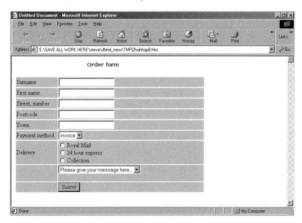

TIP

If you would like to edit a form box, open the Property Inspector by double clicking on the element.

Text boxes

Using the ⬚ button in the Object manager, insert a text field. As described earlier, you will find the corresponding command in the menu bar under INSERT/FORM OBJECTS.

After you have inserted a text field in the form, assign the necessary properties to it. Use the Property Inspector to do so.

Enter the type of text box by activating the corresponding radio button in the Property Inspector.

There are three types of text boxes:

- **Single line:** ⬚
- **Multi line:**
  Please input your message here...
- **Password:** ░░░░ The stars will be displayed after the password has been typed in. A simple text box is shown.

> **NOTE**
>
> *Unfortunately, you cannot alter the size of form elements by pulling them. Enter the line width in the corresponding box in the Property Inspector.*

In single and multi-line text boxes, you can enter any kind of text (letters, numbers). These can be displayed as single line, multiple lines or with stars (password text box).

If you want to limit the number of possible characters in a text box, enter the corresponding value in the MAX CHARS box in the Property Inspector. By doing so, you have better control over the input. British postcodes, for example, consist of no more than seven characters.

You can include an initial value in the text box.

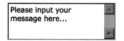

215

However, many users might think they can just enter nothing. This text cannot always be typed over either. You are better off giving an explanation of the text box either in front of it or behind.

In multi-line text boxes, you can determine whether and how a line break should be possible:

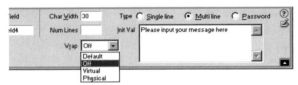

Default: Corresponds to the default setting of the browser.

Off: Suppresses all line breaks.

Virtual: The text is displayed on the screen with line breaks, but no line breaks are inserted in the input.

Physical: Line breaks appear in the input as well.

> **NOTE**
>
> *Name your form elements. You can then find your way more easily in the source code. You can also clearly arrange received information in folders. If you would like to use JavaScript, you need to assign names anyway.*

Buttons to send and reset

There are two types of buttons with which you can send the data of a form or reset the form: text and image buttons.

After inserting a **text button** in the form, define the function it is to perform in the Property Inspector.

The left text button sends the input data, for example, via e-mail to the given address.

The right button resets the form and at the same deletes all the information that the user has input.

In the Property Inspector, give the description and the function of this text button:

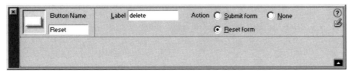

The inserted image buttons could also be filled with send and delete functions:

1 Open the HTML Source Editor.

2 Replace the code of the button with the following:

```
<button type="submit" name="send" value="value">
<img src="send.gif"></button>
```

or

```
<button type="reset" name="delete" value="value">
<img src="delete.gif"></button>
```

> **CAUTION**
>
> *With this symbol, you keep the additional information and important notes. Not all browsers display this image button correctly. Test appearance and function first.*

The functions of the buttons are both connected with the images.

> **TIP**
>
> *According to a Web convention, the send button is always placed to the left of the delete button.*

Check boxes

Check boxes are frequently used in a form to let the user select criteria. These small square boxes permit the simultaneous checking of several properties.

TIP

Name check boxes and radio buttons as well.

Radio buttons

Radio buttons are used if the user will only make one selection. If the user marks a button, the marking on another one will be lifted.

You carry out this yes/no assignment by giving the same name to the whole group.

TIP

If one of the radio buttons will appear marked at first, you will have to determine this in the Property Inspector. The user can always lift the marking by choosing another radio button.

Drop-down menus and selection lists

You differentiate between drop-down menus, where the user can only make one statement, and a list, where several entries can be selected simultaneously.

A scrollbar menu is displayed in the selection list. The selection list can either be laid out as a one-line or a multi-line list box (on the left).

The drop-down menu comes up (to the right) if the user clicks on the arrow. In a drop-down menu, only one selection is possible.

How to create a list:

1 Mark the place where you have inserted the list element in your form (see page 213).

2 Click on the LIST VALUES button in the Property Inspector.

The LIST VALUES dialog window appears.

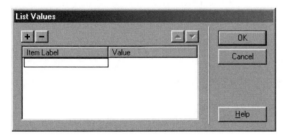

3 The cursor blinks on the place where you can insert the first entry. Type in the first list element.

4 To be able to enter more elements, click on the (+) button.

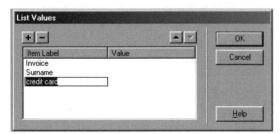

5 If you want to delete an entry, mark it and then click on (–).

6 Change the order of the list with the arrow key.

7 When you are done, click on OK.

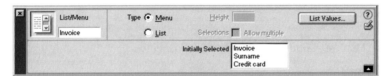

You can see the properties of a list here. Activate the corresponding check boxes if the user can select several predefined entries. You can also determine whether an entry should be highlighted by default, and the user can then alter this. Here you can also determine the height of a list.

Inserting file fields

Using this field, the user can search for files on your hard disk and send them as table data.

As described, insert a file field with the button 🗋 (see the section: Form elements). An empty text box and a button are inserted in the design view.

> NOTE
>
> *If you want to insert a file field, the method of the form must be set to* POST.

Hidden form fields

You need these elements if you want to retrieve further information (such as from the form) besides the data the user has typed in.

An example:

Of course, if you look at several Web sites, it is important to know who has filled in which form. The hidden form field provides the necessary information about URLs, form versions or similar.

> NOTE
>
> *You cannot see the hidden formula field in the browser. The values you have given are sent with the form data.*
>
> *In addition, you must have the following entry in the <form> tag:*
>
> ```
> ENCTYPE="multipart/form-data"
> ```

Jump menus

Jump menus define where a user should end up when he/she clicks on a specific entry. Using this list, or the pop-up menu, you can link to another Web site or document. Dreamweaver automatically creates the JavaScript which runs behind this for you.

1 Click on the JUMP MENU ![icon] button or on the entry under INSERT/FORM OBJECTS/ JUMP MENU. The INSERT JUMP MENU dialog window appears.

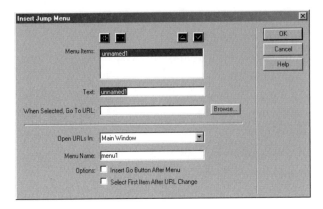

2 Enter the text for the individual selection criteria in the drop-down menu in the browser (see Drop-down menus and selection lists on page 218). Use the TEXT text box to do this.

3 Then determine the URL to be loaded: OPEN URLS IN (you can find further information about this in Chapter 5, Defining targets and in Chapter 7, Defining targets).

4 Your input is automatically taken on in the MENU ITEMS box.

5 To input other objects, click on (+); if you want to delete some, click on (–). You can also alter the order of the selection criteria later on in the drop-down menu displayed.

6 Determine further properties of these jumps. If you enter the option INSERT GO TO BUTTON AFTER MENU, the user will need to confirm the jump first.

| unnamed1 ▼ | Go |

If the check boxes remain inactive, the button will not be displayed and the target data jumps up.

7 Click on OK.

> **TIP**
>
> *Highlight the Jump menu. In the Property Inspector, you can determine its appearance: choose between drop-down menu and list boxes.*

> **NOTE**
>
> *You can also insert form elements in an HTML document where there are no <form> tags present – meaning that no form has been created yet. Confirm this to ensure the functionality of the object.*

Processing forms

The HTML source code determines the appearance of forms. In addition to this, it implements a script (such as CGI), which reprocesses this and codes the entered data on the server pages. Using Dreamweaver, you can create forms, but not scripts.

How to determine the properties of a form:

1 Highlight the form by clicking on the red lines in the document window.

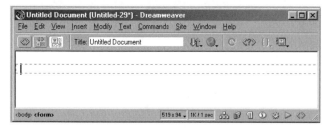

2 Determine the name of the form in the Property Inspector. Determine the executing actions and methods.

Write the URL of the script in the ACTION box, or specify an e-mail address.

> **NOTE**
>
> *General form properties are saved in the code within the <form> tags.*

223

In the `<form>` tags, you can determine how the form should be processed. Here you can, for example, name the URLs of the CGI scripts, which reprocesses the data. You can then choose between two methods:

GET: The data is sent to the specified URL, where it is saved. The CGI program must read and edit the content.

Do not use GET for long forms with extensive amounts of data.

POST: The data is provided on the server computer. The CGI program is then treated as user input, which is executed with the command line.

Your system administrator will gladly help you with this.

TIPS

- *You will also be able to send simple forms by e-mail. To do this, write the e-mail command in page 147). Example:* `mailto:"info@cybertechnics.co.uk"`

- *Name the form elements clearly. This is the only way that will allow you to evaluate the sent form data clearly and arrange the fields.*

- *It is always very good to create a confirmation page for the user. The user then knows that the form has been sent. You can create this page in the normal way in Dreamweaver. The script on the server takes care of calling the page. You may need to ask your administrator.*

- *Form input can be checked with JavaScript. For example, every e-mail must contain the @ character. If this is not the case, JavaScript generates an error message.*

Chapter 9

Layers

Web designers love layers, because they allow you to position elements any way you like on the Web site. Your Web site then becomes more dynamic and you have greater control over the elements on your page. In addition, you can hide layers and assign behaviours to them. This chapter will show you how to create layers very easily. Layers can be created within other layers; you can also overlap them. In addition, it can depend on another layer whether a level is visible or hidden.

Creating layers

Layers can be created both in the layout and in the standard view.

1 Click on the layer button 🔳 in the Object manager (on the COMMON panel).

2 In the document window, click where you want to place a corner of a layer. Drag the layer while pressing the mouse button.

The layer then turns into a cross-line.

3 Release the mouse button. The layer is created. The layer marking shows that the information has been taken on by the source code.

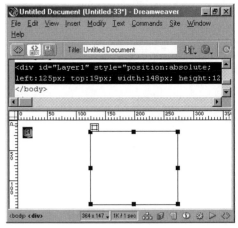

Or:

1 In the document, click where you want to insert the layer.

2 Select the INSERT/LAYER entry in the menu bar.

227

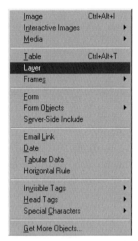

The layer is inserted in a default size. You can alter this default width and height in PREFERENCES (see HTML and layer preferences on page 248).

TIPS

- *You can insert as many layers as you want.*

- *If you don't want these to overlap, select MODIFY/ARRANGE/ PREVENT LAYER OVERLAPS.*

The inserted layer has the same handles as an image. You can alter the size using these. If you pull one of the corner handles, you can alter the height and width at the same time.

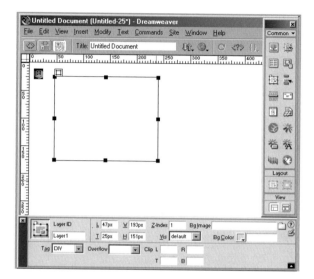

TIPS

- *The invisible icon shows that a layer has been created. Activate* 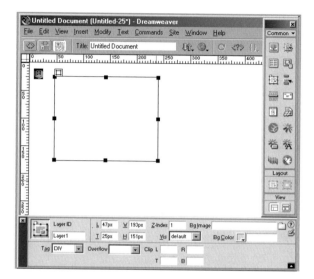 *in the PREFERENCES dialog window under EDIT/PREFERENCES/ INVISIBLE ELEMENTS so that you can open them. Activate VIEW/ VISUAL AIDS/ INVISIBLE ELEMENTS.*

- *Also activate VIEW/VISUAL AIDS/LAYER BORDERS and INVISIBLE ELEMENTS. It is then easier to change the position and size of a layer in the document window. The layer borders are not visible in the browser.*

Layer panels

You can exclude overlaps with the layer panel, change the visibility of a layer, nest layers or change the stacking order.

To show the layer panel, select WINDOW/LAYER or press F2.

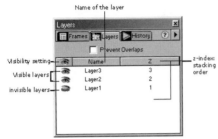

Name of the layer

Visibility setting
Visible layers
invisible layers

z-index stacking order

All of the single layers are listed in the panel. If you create a new layer, the existing ones move one position below in the list.

The Z index

The Z index determines whether a layer is stacked over or under another.

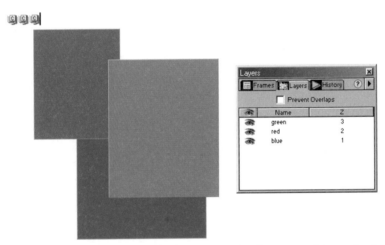

The **green layer** with the Z index 3 is stacked on top of the **red** with the value 2, which again is on top of the **blue** with value 1.

How to change the stacking order of layers (or the Z value):

1 Select the corresponding layer in the LAYER panel (see Marking a layer on page 235).

2 Move the layer to the correct position in the panel.

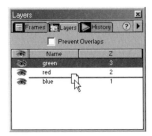

3 The Z value changes.

Or, directly assign the Z value:

1 Mark the layer in the layers window. Click roughly in the middle of the line.

The name and the Z index are now marked separately.

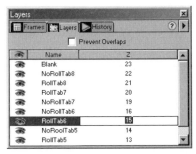

The Z values are sorted in increasing order. The upper layer is also the layer above the others in the document window. If you want to change the stacking order, move the layers to the desired place or manually type in the new Z value.

2 Type in a new value for the Z index in the Layer window.

Or, enter the new Z value in the Z INDEX text box in the Property Inspector.

Confirm with ⏎. The layer is now moved to the corresponding place in the LAYER window.

Nested layers

You can place a layer within another layer. A layer group arises from this. The position and visibility of the nested layer is then dependent on the primary layer.

1 In the existing layer, click where you want to insert the sub layer.

2 Select INSERT/LAYER in the menu bar.

Or:

1 Move the INSERT LAYER 📇 from the Object manager to the existing layer.

Or:

1 Highlight the layer you want to integrate into another in the LAYER panel.

2 Move this layer to the corresponding entry of the other one. Press the Ctrl (Windows) or ⌘ (Macintosh) key.

3 Release the mouse button if you see a frame around the name of the target layer.

You now see the nested layer at the + character.

A nested layer is inserted in the **green** layer. Click on + to see the sub layers in the Layer panel.

CAUTION

If you have activated PREVENT OVERLAPS in the LAYER panel, you are not able to see the nested layers.

How to cancel a nesting:

- Click on the name of the layer in the LAYER window and move it to the desired position. If the layer is not visible, click on the + character in the LAYER window or select the layer in the document window.

  Depending on the properties the layer has assigned to it, the position of the layer may change.

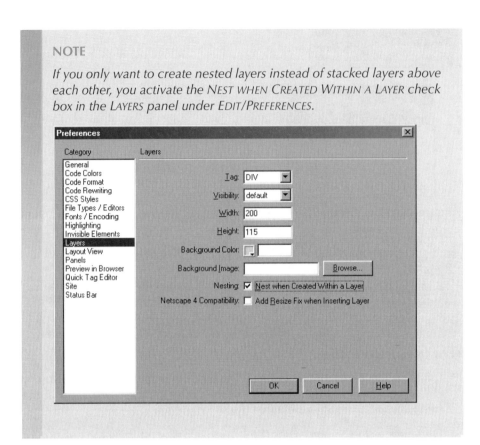

Inserting content

If you would like to insert content in a layer, click on the layer in the document window. In this now activated layer you can insert text, images, tables, and other page elements. The only thing you cannot insert is frames. And you can only use one frame per layer.

You can format these elements in the usual way. You can also use Cascading Style Sheets.

Layer properties

As well as the stacking order (see The Z index on page 230) you have the option of altering size, alignment, background and visibility of a layer.

Marking a layer

You can mark a layer by

- clicking on the name in the Layer window, or
- clicking on the layer border, or
- clicking on the marking handle of the individual layer, or
- clicking on the layer marking (must be activated to be visible under EDIT/VISUAL AIDS/INVISIBLE ELEMENTS), or
- clicking on the layer with a depressed ⏎ key, or
- clicking on `<span>`, `<div>`, `<layer>` or `<ilayer>` in the Tag Selector.

> **TIP**
>
> *Mark several layers at the same time by pressing the ⏎ key. Then proceed as described above.*

A marked layer is shown with the invisible icon and the layer symbol. The entry is marked in the LAYER window. Drag one of the eight handles to change the size of the layer.

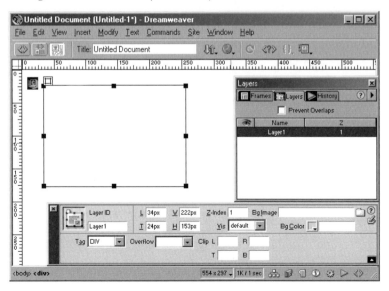

Naming a layer

To be able to assign definite behaviours to a layer later, the layers must be clearly named. By default, Dreamweaver names the layers as Layer 1, Layer 2, Layer 3, etc.

It is also easier to work with several layers when they are clearly named.

1 Mark the layer (see page 235).

2 Type in the name of the layer in the LAYER ID text box in the Property Inspector.

Only use alphanumerical characters. Blank spaces, hyphens, slashes and numbers by themselves are not allowed.

Or, double click on the name in the Layer panel and overwrite the default name.

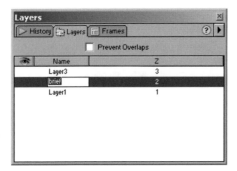

Changing the size

You can alter the width or height of one or several layers at the same time.

> **TIP**
>
> *If you exclude the overlapping of layers in the* LAYER *panel, you can only alter the size of a layer to where it meets the border of another one (see Layer panels on page 229).*

How to alter the size of a layer:

1 Mark the layer (see Marking a layer on page 235).

2 Pull the handles until you have reached the desired width and height.

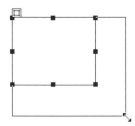

> **TIP**
>
> *To alter width and height at the same time, pull a corner handle.*

If you enlarge or reduce the layers in small steps, use the arrow key and press the Ctrl key down.

Or:

Type in the new values in the W (width) and H (height) text boxes in the Property Inspector.

How to alter the size of more than one layer at the same time:

1 Mark the layer.

2 Select MODIFY/ALIGN/MAKE SAME WIDTH or MODIFY/ALIGN/MAKE SAME HEIGHT.

All the layers now have the same size. The size of the largest layer is assigned to the others.

Or:

Determine the new values for the width and the height in the Property Inspector. By default, Dreamweaver interprets the entry in pixels (px), but you can also enter them as pc (picas), pt (points), in (inches), mm (millimetres), cm (centimetres) or % (percentage of the primary layer or, for example, the page). There should be no blank spaces between the value and the measurement.

Positioning layers

If you have worked with a photo editing program before, you already know the basics.

> **CAUTION**
>
> *If you would like to move a layer underneath or on top of another, the Prevent Overlaps check box must be deactivated (see Layer panels on page 229).*

1 Mark the layer.

2 Move the layer to the desired position with the mouse.

Or:

Use the arrow keys.

Or:

Type in the new X and Y values in the L (left) and T (top) boxes of the Property Inspector.

These results refer to the nested layers on the primary levels which are otherwise on the upper left corner of the page.

> **NOTE**
>
> *By default, Dreamweaver sets the position values in pixels. To use other values, you will need to enter the measurement unit next to the value.*
>
> *You can also enter the X and Y values in other units. However, you need to type these in. If you do not set the units, Dreamweaver will interpret the input in pixels.*

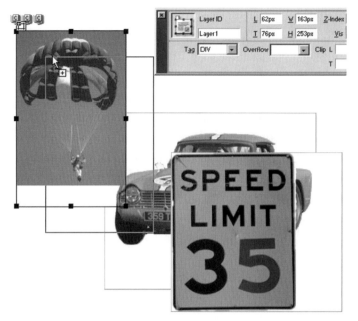

In this example, layer 1 (with the parachute image) is dragged to a new position with the mouse. Pay attention to the Property Inspector when moving the layer. The new coordinates are shown at the same time.

Absolute, relative and static position:

In HTML, layers can be positioned absolute, relative or static:

- **Static positioning:** Browsers that do not support layers integrate the elements in the surrounding page contents. These browsers define the <div> tags as paragraph breaks and the <span> tag as a line break.

- **Absolute positioning:** The layer is positioned in relation to the left upper corner of the page or the primary layer. The <div> tag causes a paragraph break in the primary layer or in the HTML page.

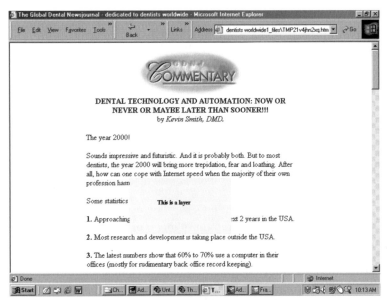

In this example, the layer will be inserted on the HTML page after the text string "The year 2000!". In the browser, a line break will appear in this place.

- **Relative positioning:** Use the `<span>` tag to ensure the line position of the primary levels or the HTML page.

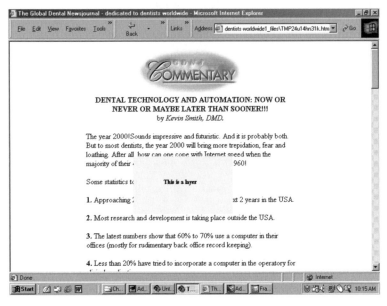

This layer is inserted with the `<span>` tag. Apart from this, nothing is changed in the source code. The line position of the primary text has not changed at all. The layer floats about independently of this.

How to change the tag:

1 Mark the layer.

2 Select the desired tag entry from the drop-down menu of the Property Inspector.

Aligning layers

You can only align layers in relation to each other. The last marked layer then forms the base for the orientation of the others.

1 Mark two or more layers that you want to align to each other.

2 Select the desired alignment under MODIFY/ALIGN.

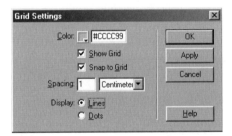

In this example, all the layers are aligned on the baseline.

How to align layers to the grid:

The grid simply makes it possible for you to position the layers accurately (see Chapter 1).

1 Select VIEW/GRID/EDIT GRID.

2 Determine the measurement unit (SPACING) for the grid and activate SNAP TO GRID. Activate the SHOW GRID check box.

3 Mark the layer to position and move it to the desired position.

The layer now snaps to the closest grid point.

> NOTE
>
> *The aligning to the grid also works when the grid is not visible.*

Determining the background

You can assign a background colour or a background image.

1 Select the layer.

2 Determine the colour for the background in the Property Inspector.

Proceed as shown in Chapter 2, Page properties and The background.

> **TIPS**
>
> - *Do not specify a background colour if the layer is supposed to stay transparent.*
>
> - *Using style presentations, you can assign further attributes to the background image.*
>
> - *Define a tracing image in the PAGE PROPERTIES dialog box. Set the image transparency to about 40% to 60%. Now you can build the layers according to the image.*
>
> - *If you wish to change the position of the tracing image, select VIEW/ TRACING IMAGE/ADJUST POSITION. Enter the new x and y values in the dialog window or move the image to the desired position with the arrow key. The dialog window must remain open for this.*

Visibility

Depending on which area you work in, it can seem reasonable to remove other layers first. This is a great help, even with encapsulated or overlapping layers.

At first, an invisible level is not shown after loading the page. However, when a specific action is executed, the hidden layer is displayed.

The closed eye 👁 symbolises the hidden layer.

The open eye ![eye] stands for a visible layer.

If no symbol is available, the properties of the primary level are accepted.

How to alter the visibility of the layers:

- In the left column of the LAYER window, click until the desired status is shown.

- If all the layers are supposed to be visible or hidden, click on the eye in the bar above.

Or:

- Select an option from the VISIBILITY drop-down menu in the Property Inspector:

Default: Most browsers interpret this as INHERIT.

Inherit: The qualities of the primary level are taken on.

Visible: Layer visible.

Hidden: Layer hidden.

> **TIP**
>
> *You can assign a definite behaviour to a (hidden) layer (![icon]). Use the timeline or the Behaviour Inspector for this. You can, for example, control the visibility of a layer with JavaScript.*

Overflow of the content

Determine the behaviours of a layer in the Property Inspector whose contents go beyond the limits of the layer. This area can be opened with VISIBLE, HIDDEN, AUTO or SCROLL.

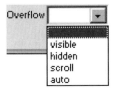

CAUTION

It is only Internet Explorer that can interpret the SCROLL option.

If you activate AUTO, Internet Explorer will interpret these as scrollbars; Netscape converts the option with HIDDEN.

In this example, the image is larger than the layer. SCROLL is entered in the Property Inspector. However, only Internet Explorer can interpret this setting. In Netscape, the image will be cut to the layer size:

Clipped areas

You can make only a specific part of the layer visible. You determine this area in the Property Inspector:

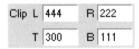

You type in the values for the clipping of a layer. By doing so, you define a rectangle.

In the following figure, the same image is integrated in the layer as above:

HTML and layer preferences

Layers are installed on the page with the following tags: <div>, <span>, <layer>, <ilayer>.

Although most browsers can only interpret the <div> and <span> tags by default, Dreamweaver creates a layer with <div>.

Netscape 4 or higher are the only browsers to display <layer> and <ilayer>.

Example:

```
<div id="Layer1" style="position:absolute;
visibility:inherit; width:180px; height:85px; z-index:1">
</div>
```

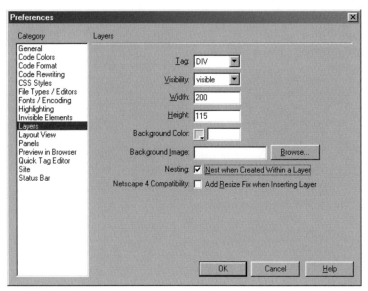

The layer settings determine which tags should be used. Establish other general settings for the default layer.

How to change the layer preferences:

1 Select the LAYER category under EDIT/PREFERENCES.

2 Determine which tag should be inserted in the layer.

3 Set the visibility (see page 244).

4 Width and height refer to the default layer, which you determine by going to INSERT/LAYER in the menu bar.

5 You can determine the background colour or a background image for the default layer.

6 Layers stacked on top of others could be set to HIDDEN by default.

7 Insert JavaScript on the page with the ADD RESIZE FIX WHEN INSERTING LAYER (NETSCAPE 4 COMPATIBILITY) option, which eliminates a bug in Netscape. If you enlarge or reduce the navigation window, layers will be wrongly interpreted. With this script, the problem is overcome by reloading the page.

249

Converting layers into tables (and vice versa)

Layers can be converted to HTML. Older versions (before the 4th generation) possibly still display the contents of a layer, but cannot interpret the positioning (and the Z index).

How to convert layers into tables:

1 Select FILE/CONVERT/3.0 BROWSER COMPATIBLE. The CONVERT TO 3.0 BROWSER COMPATIBLE dialog box appears.

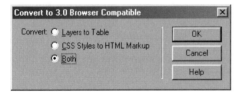

2 If you select the LAYERS TO TABLE option, all the layers will be replaced by a single table, which keeps its original size.

3 If you have used CSS Styles, these should also be converted. To do this, select the check box BOTH.

4 Click on OK. Dreamweaver creates a document that can be read correctly by older browsers.

TIP

If layers are used in connection with tables, first select the layers and convert these into tables. In Dreamweaver 4, you can also use the tools in the layout mode.

CAUTION

Dreamweaver cannot convert nested or overlapping layers into tables.

How to convert tables into layers:

January						
1	2	3	4	5	6	7
8	9	10	11	12	13	14
15	16	17	18	19	20	21
22	23	24	25	26	27	28
29	30	31				

This table will be converted in the following steps:

1 Select MODIFY/CONVERT/TABLES TO LAYERS.

2 Set the desired options for the layers to be created in the CONVERT TABLES TO LAYERS dialog window.

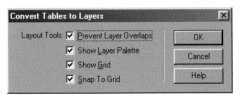

3 Press the OK button. Each table cell is converted into a layer.

CAUTION

- *You are only able to convert layers into tables or tables into layers for an entire page, not individual page elements.*

- *Dreamweaver does not create a new HTML document during the conversion. So, be very careful when saving!*

Chapter 10

Behaviours

In Dreamweaver, you can quickly and easily integrate interactive elements into your page. Depending on what the user does, and which events occur, certain actions will be executed. Elements can also be altered automatically. In this chapter, you will learn how to apply interactive elements. First, we will discuss the timeline, and then move on to JavaScript commands and multimedia elements, which I will explain in more detail in the next workshop.

The timeline

Using the timeline, you can create DHTML, with which the properties of layers and images can be temporarily changed. You can alter the position (movement), size, visibility and the stacking order of layers. You can also change the source of an image temporarily and, by doing so, provide the user with an insight into a whole photo album. Behaviours, as objects, can be influenced.

WHAT IS THIS?

*Dynamic HTML (**DHTML**) is based on JavaScript, CSS and HTML. Browsers of Version 4.0 interpret Dynamic HTML – though quite dissimilarly.*

NOTE

The source code inserted with the timeline is encapsulated in the MM_initTimelines *function within the* <head>.

The Timeline Inspector

You can determine properties of layers and images in the timeline with the Timeline Inspector.

To open the timeline, select WINDOW/TIMELINE in the menu bar. Alternatively, press ⇧ + F9.

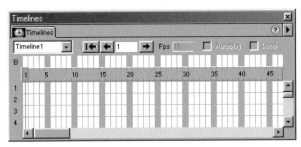

In the top row of the Timeline Inspector there are buttons with which you can control the playing of the animation.

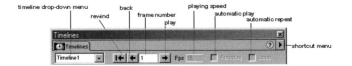

timeline drop-down menu   back   playing speed
rewind   frame number   automatic play
play   automatic repeat

> **NOTE**
>
> *The timeline is only active when the design view is activated. Therefore, click on the layout window.*

If you have created more than one timeline, you can select them from the TIMELINES drop-down menu.

If you would like to view the whole animation in Dreamweaver, press the PLAY button ➡. To go on to the next frame, click once on the PLAY button.

Depending on how many frames are to be played per second (Bps; playback speed), the animation will run quickly or slowly. The default speed is 15 Bps.

Press the BACK button to return to the previous frame. If you want to return to the beginning of the animation, use the REWIND button.

The PLAYBACK HEAD is always in the position which is currently displayed in the document window. The current frame is displayed in the FRAME NUMBER.

The AUTO PLAY check box inserts a behaviour into the source code, which determines that the timeline is played as soon as the page is loaded.

If the check box Loop is activated, a behaviour is displayed in the Behaviours Channel. If the animation was played, this is immediately restarted and played in further loops. You can decide how often the animation should be played. You will find further information in the Behaviours section on page 263.

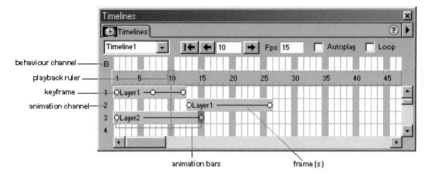

behaviour channel
playback ruler
keyframe
animation channel

animation bars — frame(s)

You can insert further behaviours (see page 264) in the BEHAVIOURS CHANNEL, which is called from a specific frame.

Every object which is included in the animation and is displayed symbolically using the ANIMATION BARS in the timeline is saved in a separate ANIMATIONS CHANNEL.

The animation bar consists of several FRAMES. A **frame** is a scene of the animation.

> CAUTION
>
> *These are not the same frames as in Chapter 7.*

A KEY FRAME is a key scene assigned with specified properties. During the playing, Dreamweaver alters these properties and a certain dynamicity is generated. Normal frames are placed between two key frames, so that these changes in the properties will be executed more fluently by Dreamweaver.

In the timeline, frames and key frames will be represented by a small box or a numbered column. In addition, the key frame has a small circle. Behaviours can only be assigned to key frames.

Creating an animation

The timeline can only control layers Chapter 9).

How to animate a layer:

1 Move the layer to the position where you want it to be placed in the first frame of the animation. Keep the layer highlighted.

2 Select MODIFY>TIMELINE/ADD OBJECT TO TIMELINE in the menu bar.

Or pull the object (the layer) into the timeline. A bar with the name of the layer appears in the animation channel of the timeline.

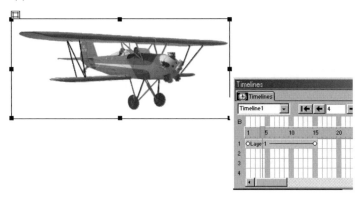

3 Click in the key frame at the end of the bar. The controller automatically changes its position.

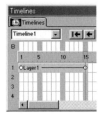

4 Move the layer to where you want it to be at the last setting of the animation.

A line shows the course of the animation.

5 If the animation runs in a curve, you will have to insert more key frames. To do this, right click in the middle area of the animation bar. The context menu opens.

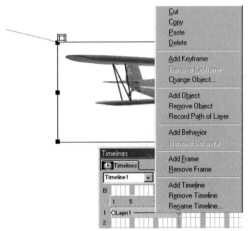

You will learn more about how to create complex animations below.

6 Select ADD KEYFRAME in the context menu.

Or, right click in the frame and, at the same time, press the [Ctrl] key (Windows) or the [⌘] key (Macintosh).

Repeat these steps to insert further key frames.

> **TIP**
>
> *In the context menu, you will find all the commands required to edit the animations. You will find the same commands in the shortcut menu as in the TIMELINES panel.*

7 Click on the key frame or place the controller on the frame. Change the position of the layer.

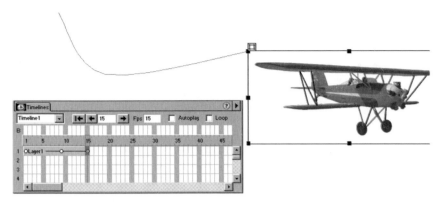

In this example, the plane flies in a curve.

8 Repeat steps 1 to 7 to animate further layers.

> **CAUTION**
>
> *Changes in the layer attributes width and height using the timeline are not displayed by Netscape 4.*

How to create animations with complex paths:

1 Select the layer and place it where you want it to appear in the first animation frame (see above).

2 Select MODIFY/TIMELINES/RECORD PATH OF LAYER.

3 Pull the layer over the page by pressing the mouse button. Draw the path with this motion. Release the mouse button when you have created the path.

In the timeline, more key frames were inserted in the animation bar.

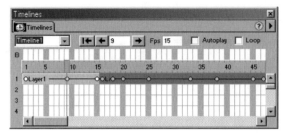

4 Click on the REWIND button in the timeline and start the animation by pressing the PLAY button.

> **TIP**
>
> *You can make further changes after you have created an animation bar. You can, for example, add or delete frames, or move the start point of an animation. Use the context or the shortcut menu.*

Changing other layer attributes:

1 Include the layers in the timeline. If required, add key frames. Proceed as described above.

2 Select the key frame whose properties you want to alter. Using the left mouse button, click on this key frame to do this.

3 Alter the attribute in the LAYER panel and/or in the Property Inspector.

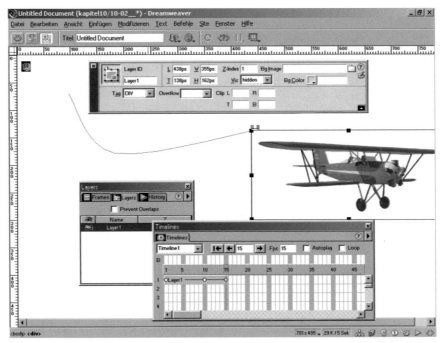

For example, enter a new Z index, alter the size of the layer or determine whether a layer should be visible or hidden.

4 Press the PLAY button to check the result.

TIP

You can also control the visibility of a layer with JavaScript. To do this, use the Behaviour Inspector.

How to animate an image:

1 Position the image in the document window.

2 Drag the image into the timeline or select ADD OBJECT in the shortcut menu. The animation bar of the image will be inserted in the channel in the timeline.

3 Click on the right end of the bar in the last key frame.

4 Open the Property Inspector.

5 Name the source of the image that should be displayed in this frame.

6 To display additional images, you will have to insert further images. Proceed as described from step 4.

> **TIP**
>
> *If the loading time becomes longer, it makes more sense to work with visible and hidden layers. All the images will then be loaded at once and can be played regularly.*

How to edit the animation:

- If the animation is to be played for longer, move the last key frame more to the right, or the first key frame further to the left. The proportional distance between the individual key frames will be kept.

- If the animation is to be shorter, move the last key frame to the left, or the first key frame to the right.

- If the animation is to start at another point in time, select the whole of the animation bar by clicking on it. Move it to the desired position. You can select several bars by pressing the ⇧ key. If you would like the animation to start later, move the bar to the right; if it should start earlier, move it to the left.

- Key frames within the animation can be pushed back and forth until you achieve the desired effect.

- To alter the entire position of the animation, select the animation bar and move layer and path to the desired position in the document window.

- Use the command MODIFY/TIMELINES/ADD FRAME to add more frames. You delete a frame in the timeline with MODIFY/TIMELINES/DELETE FRAME. You can also use the corresponding entry in the shortcut bar or in the context menu.

> **TIP**
>
> *If your page contains more actions, you should create different timelines. Select MODIFY/TIMELINES/ADD TIMELINE.*

Behaviours

As already indicated, you can define definite actions in the timeline. If you have assigned a behaviour to a frame within an animation, a bar appears in the behaviours channel.

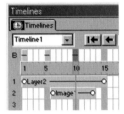

WHAT IS THIS?

*By **behaviour**, we understand the carrying out of a concrete action, as soon as a definite event has arisen. Particular prerequisites must also be fulfilled before a behaviour can be carried out. The user causes these events in the browser if he/she moves the mouse or clicks on something, for example. If the browser recognises that a definite action is intended for this event, it executes the corresponding JavaScript.*

NOTE

- *You can also assign behaviours to other objects on the Web site. Simple layers, images and links count as these.*

- *Not all browsers support JavaScript. In addition, users can have their JavaScript option on the browser deactivated. However, you can still offer this user a page that works with the <noscript> tag.*

- *You can control the timeline with JavaScript commands in the browser later. You can, for example, call up a specific frame, rewind the bar or put the animation on hold. You will find the corresponding command in the Behaviour Inspector (see page 264).*

- *Assign definite behaviours to your page if you want to make it possible for the user to act interactively.*

The Behaviour Inspector

Using the Behaviour Inspector, you can assign a concrete action to a definite event. Dreamweaver offers a panel of events and automatically displays the related JavaScript commands. This means that you do not need to have any knowledge of JavaScript to develop an interactive page in Dreamweaver.

Open the Behaviour Inspector using WINDOW/BEHAVIOURS

or click on the [icon] button in the Launcher

or press ⇧ + F3.

The selected tag appears in the title bar of the Behaviour Inspector. In the following example, the events and actions are connected with the <a> tag in the Behaviour Inspector.

Behaviours that are assigned to definite elements are listed in the Behaviour Inspector.

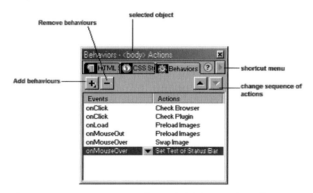

The events are arranged in alphabetical order. Several actions are assigned to one event, these will appear in the order the browser is to process them.

Adding a behaviour

You can assign a behaviour to either the complete document (the <body> tag) or to single page elements, such as images.

Whether a definite event arises, or the object fulfils a concrete prerequisite, an action defined for this is executed:

Object + event = action

How to assign a behaviour to an element:

1 Select the element in the document window. If you would like to assign a behaviour to the whole document, click on <body> in the Tag Selector.

2 Click on the (+) character in the Behaviour Inspector. The drop-down action menu appears.

Call JavaScript
Change Property
Check Browser
Check Plugin
Control Shockwave or Flash
Drag Layer
Go To URL
Jump Menu
Jump Menu Go
Open Browser Window
Play Sound
Popup Message
Preload Images
Set Nav Bar Image
Set Text ▶
Show-Hide Layers
Swap Image
Swap Image Restore
Timeline ▶
Validate Form

Show Events For ▶

Get More Behaviors...

3 Select the desired action.

4 A dialog window appears in which you can establish further parameters for these actions. Establish these and confirm with OK.

> **NOTE**
>
> *You can assign several actions to an event. To alter the order of the actions, select these and then click on the arrow keys ▲▼ in the Behaviour Inspector. You can only alter the order of actions within an event. Events are always ordered alphabetically in the Inspector.*

> **CAUTION**
>
> *The older the browser version, the fewer behaviours the browser can execute.*

How to create a rollover image:

1 Click on 🖼 in the Object manager.

Or, select INSERT/INTERACTIVE IMAGES/ROLLOVER IMAGE in the menu bar.

Or, press the 🖼 button in the Object manager.

Or, select INSERT/INTERACTIVE IMAGES/NAVIGATION BAR to create a complex navigation bar.

The INSERT ROLLOVER IMAGE dialog box or the INSERT NAVIGATION BAR will then appear.

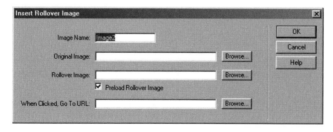

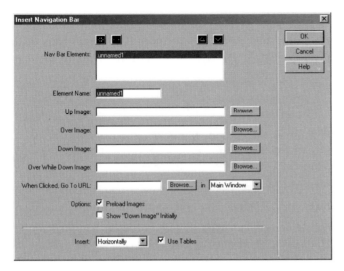

2 Enter the source for the original and the rollover image and assign an image name.

3 Determine with which page the inserted link should be connected.

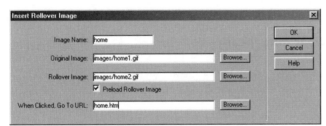

4 Confirm your entry with OK.

> **CAUTION**
>
> *Pay attention to the image size of the rollover images. Width and height of the original image are taken on from the rollover image. If the original and the rollover image are different sizes, there will be some distortion.*

Behaviours and text:

You cannot assign behaviours to text blocks, although some actions and events can be connected to text links. Therefore, you must first put in a dummy link:

1 Select the text area.

2 Type in # in the LINK text box in the Property Inspector.

3 Assign a behaviour to this link with the Behaviour Inspector.

> **TIP**
>
> *Instead of the # character, you can also enter "javascript:;" in the text field. Type in the quotation marks and include semicolon and colon.*

> **NOTE**
>
> *To prevent the text link from being underlined, use the CSS command:*
> `style="text-decoration:none"`

How to delete a behaviour from the list:

1 In the Property Inspector, select the event or the action that you want to delete by clicking on the corresponding entry in the Behaviour Inspector.

2 Click on the (–) key. The entry is deleted from the list.

TIPS

- *To alter an event afterwards, click on the arrow key in the lower text box.*

- *If you would like to delete the behaviours, mark the entry and then click on the (–) character.*

TIP

An event is listed in brackets (e.g. onClick). These function only if a link is available. In the Property Inspector, you can see that Dreamweaver has inserted a dummy #, provided that no link is available yet. Determine where the link should be inserted. If you delete the # character, you also remove the behaviour that is attached to it.

Altering a behaviour

You can assign new actions or parameters to individual events.

- If you would like to alter the **event**, double click on the entry in the Behaviour Inspector. Click on the events and actions in the lower text box. Determine the new event in the menu that opens.

- To alter an **action**, mark the entry in the Behaviour Inspector. Or, select the entry and then press the ⏎ key. Then, alter the parameter in the dialog box.

- If you want to alter the **order of the actions** of an event, use the arrow key at the top right of the Behaviour Inspector.

TIP

You will find more behaviours on the Macromedia Web site or on a third party developer page. You can also write your own JavaScript commands and integrate them in Dreamweaver. To do this, click on the (+) button in the Behaviour Inspector. Select the GET MORE BEHAVIOURS entry in the menu that opens. The Macromedia Web page will be loaded in the primary browser, from which you can download further behaviours.

269

Chapter 11

Multimedia

In the previous chapter, you saw how a page with behaviours can be made interactive. In this workshop, we will discuss multimedia elements. A Web site becomes more interesting and lively if this aspect is added. You will learn how to insert and edit multimedia elements on the page. For this purpose, Dreamweaver 4 integrates the creation of Flash animations. In addition, in a brief overview, you will learn what you can apply from Shockwave, sound files (such as MP3), Java Applets and ActiveX. In this workshop, you will get an insight into the topic. Further information and links are to be found in the Appendix (Surf tips).

Inserting and editing media

The procedure is always the same, whether you wish to insert a Java Applet, Quick Time Movie, Flash, ActiveX or other audio and video objects on a Web page:

1 In the design window, click where you want to insert the object.

2 To insert the object, click on the corresponding button in the Object manager. The multimedia elements are distributed on two panels:

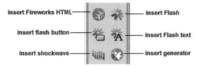

Figure 11.1: Multimedia elements on the COMMON panel in the Object manager

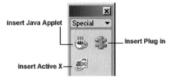

Figure 11.2: The SPECIAL panel in the Object manager

Or select INSERT/INTERACTIVE IMAGES.

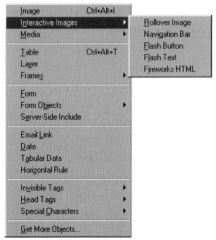

Alternatively, select the element under INSERT/MEDIA in the menu bar.

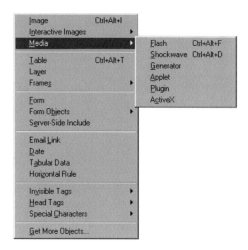

3 A dialog window opens. If you want to insert a **Shockwave** and **Flash** file, a **Java Applet** or **Netscape Plugin**, you will need to select the corresponding file in the dialog window.

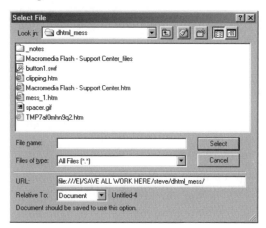

4 If you wish to integrate created HTML source code from **Fireworks** on the Web page, the INSERT FIREWORKS HTML dialog box appears.

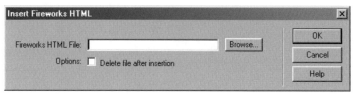

If you click on the BROWSE... button, the SELECT FILE dialog box appears.

5 If you insert **ActiveX**, at first a dummy appears in the document window:

Determine the attributes and parameters using the Properties Inspector. More information will follow.

6 Enter the directory and file name of the object to be inserted.

> **TIP**
>
> *If no dialog box appears, check whether the SHOW DIALOG WHEN INSERTING OBJECTS check box is marked and whether this option is active. This entry is found on the COMMON panel under EDIT/ PREFERENCES.*

> **NOTE**
>
> *If you insert a Flash movie on the Web page, Dreamweaver generates different tags for Netscape (<embed>) and Internet Explorer (<object>).*

Determining attributes and parameters:

1 Select the inserted object. You can determine the attributes for the object in the Property Inspector. You can determine different kinds of features, depending on which multimedia element you have marked here.

In the following example, a dummy appears for the (Flash) object in the design window. You can read and change these attributes in the Property Inspector.

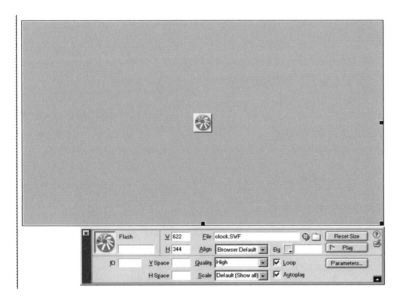

2 Click on the green PLAY key ▷ Play if you wish to look at the result of your settings in the design window.

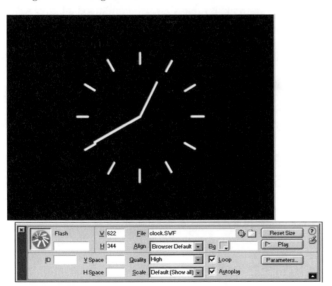

The animation will later be played like this in the browser.

3 As long as the movie or another element is played, the PLAY key in the Property Inspector becomes a red STOP key. Click on this button or select VIEW/PLUGINS/STOP or VIEW/PLUGINS/STOP ALL in the menu bar.

4 If you have selected an object where you can determine parameters (Shockwave, ActiveX, Netscape Plug in, Java Applet), a PARAMETERS [Parameters...] button will appear in the Property Inspector.

5 Press the PARAMETERS button or right click on the element. Then select the PARAMETER entry from the context menu.

6 Determine the parameter in the dialog window that now opens:

- Click on the (+) button.
- Give the name of the parameters in the PARAMETER column.
- Enter the values of the parameters in the VALUE column.
- Click on the (–) button to remove a parameter from the list.
- Alter the order with the arrow key.

Creating and inserting Flash buttons

In the previous example, we integrated an existing Flash button on the Web page. In Dreamweaver 4, you have the options of either creating Flash buttons and text objects yourself, or using those that are already available.

> **CAUTION**
>
> *You will need to save your HTML document before you can create a Flash or text button. You must also be in the layout view.*

1 Select the INSERT FLASH BUTTON from the Object manager (see Inserting and editing media on page 272) or select INSERT/INTERACTIVE IMAGES/FLASH BUTTON from the menu bar.

The INSERT FLASH BUTTON dialog box appears. Set the appearance of the buttons to be created here.

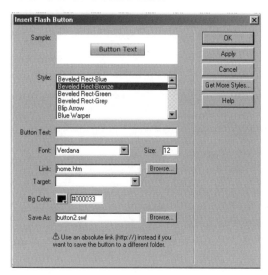

2 Determine the style of the button. You can see a preview of this in the example box above. You can move the mouse over the button and then click in order to find out how the button will work later on. However, your text inputs and formatting are not visible yet.

Sample: Button Text

3 Determine further attributes (font, size, links) of the button description.

4 Determine the directory and the name the Flash buttons should be saved under.

5 Click on OK, or press on the APPLY button if the dialog window should be opened.

Inserting Flash text

In Dreamweaver 4, you can save the text as Flash animation and install it on the Web page.

1 Press the ⚡A button in the Object manager or select INSERT/INTERACTIVE IMAGES/FLASH TEXT.

The INSERT FLASH TEXT dialog box appears.

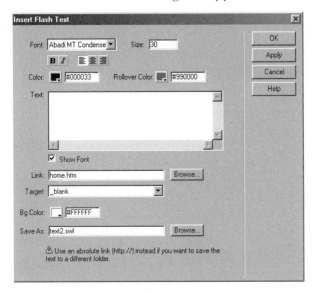

2 Select a font from the drop-down menu.

3 Determine the font size.

4 Activate style attributes like **bold** or *italic* by pressing the corresponding buttons. Determine the text alignment.

5 Determine the text colour and the colour for the rollover. Enter the hexadecimal code for this or select the desired colour from the colour palette.

6 Type in the text in the text box. Activate the SHOW FONT check box if the text in the text box is to be displayed in the selected font.

7 Determine the link that should be connected to Flash animations later on. Also determine the **target**.

8 Determine the background colour for the text.

9 Enter a file name under which the created SWF file should be saved.

10 Click on OK or APPLY TO to insert the text button on the Web page. Use the APPLY button to keep the dialog window open after inserting the animation.

The animation will automatically be created by Dreamweaver and inserted in the document window.

> **NOTE**
>
> *If you give a relative link, an error message will appear in the dialog window, saying that a Flash animation can only be displayed in the browser if this is saved in the same directory as the HTML document.*

Flash attributes

In the following section, I will introduce the two attributes QUALITY and SCALE. These two pull-down menus are characteristic of Flash movies.

Select the Flash animation in the design window. The Property Inspector only shows the features of this animation.

Other attributes such as, for example, object size, colour or object name have already been repeatedly mentioned and described in other places.

QUALITY: In this drop-down menu, you determine whether the animation should be played at high or low quality.

SCALE: With the SCALE parameter, you determine how the object should appear in the browser window if width and height are set to percentage.

The whole movie will be displayed in STANDARD. The proportions are kept in the correct ratio. Border lines can appear.

If you select NO BORDER, no border appears, but it can lead to distortions.

With the EXACT FIT option, the movie covers the whole area. The proportions of height and width can also be distorted here.

If the AUTOPLAY check box is activated, the movie will automatically be played as soon as the page is loaded.

If the LOOP check box is activated, the movie will always be played again as soon as it reaches the end.

Shockwave movies

Movies created in Macromedia Director will be inserted as Shockwave movies on the Web page. Shockwave movies inserted in Dreamweaver can be played both in Internet Explorer and in Netscape.

TIPS

- *Use Macromedia Aftershock to connect platform independent HTML and JavaScript with Shockwave movies. With Aftershock, you can, for example, check which browser or which plugin the users of your page have installed. The movies can then be adapted correspondingly. This utility is delivered together with the Director.*

- *With the help of behaviours, you can control and play Shockwave and Flash movies.*

WHAT IS THIS?

*A **plugin** is an additional module for software, installed directly in the interface. For example, Flash animations can be played only if the Shockwave plugin is installed in the browser.*

Audio

There are a number of different formats for sound files. There are two ways of integrating these in the Web page.

If you create a link to a sound file, the user can decide whether to play the sound or not.

How to connect a sound file:

1 Select the text or the image the sound should be connected to.

2 Determine the directory and the name of the audio file in the LINK text box in the Property Inspector. Proceed as described in Chapter 5.

3 Press ENTER ⏎. The selection is connected with the sound file.

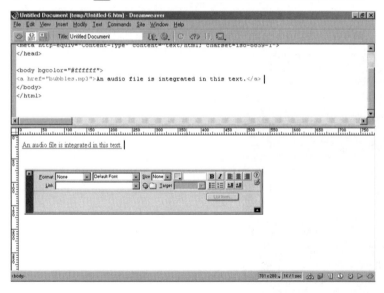

If the user of your page clicks on the link, the file will either be downloaded or played.

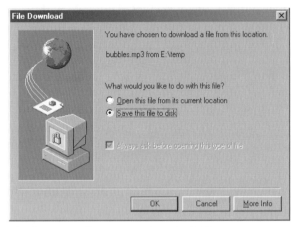

The browser then uses its own ability or accesses a plugin. Also, an external program (such as WinAmp) may start and play the sound file.

If an error message appears, it means that the browser or the plugin do not support the file type.

Another option is to integrate the audio file directly on the page. The sound will then be played as soon as it, or the Web page, is loaded. The user of your page needs the corresponding plugin for this, though. In this way, you can integrate sound on to your page if this is to be played in the background. In addition to this, you have greater control: you can control the start and the end, as well as the volume.

How to integrate sound files into the pages:

1 In the document window, select where you want to insert the sound file or the sound controller.

2 Press the PLUG-IN button ![plugin icon] in the Object manager or select INSERT/MEDIA/PLUGIN in the menu bar. The SELECT FILE dialog window appears.

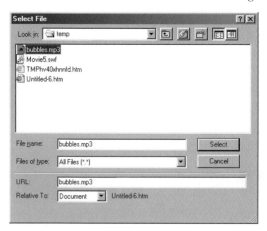

> **TIP**
>
> *You can also insert other media on the Web page using the plugin button. These are integrated in the <embed> tag, which leads to better results in Netscape. Several plugins run together with the browser or start an auxiliary application (such as Realplayer).*

3 Determine the height and width of the object in the Property Inspector.

If you wish to embed an invisible sound file, you will have to type in the following code line in the HTML Source Inspector:

```
<embed src="sound/yourfile.wav" autoplay=""true"
hidden="true"></embed>
```

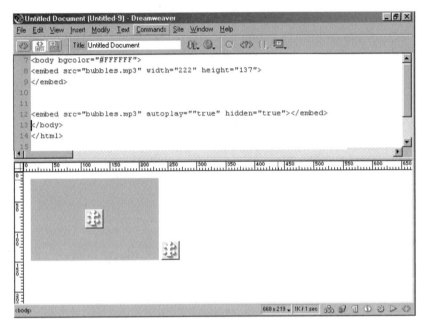

Figure 11.3: On the left, the visible sound controller is integrated, on the right, an invisible one. In the source code, you can see the corresponding attributes and parameters

4 In the Property Inspector, name the Web page where the user can download the plugin if it is not yet installed on the user's computer.

5 Click on the PLAY key or press ↵ to play the sound in the browser or the application.

> NOTE
>
> *As from Internet Explorer 4, you can install a background sound in the page:*
>
> ```
> <bgsound src="sound/yourfile.wav" loop="infinite"
> autoplay="true" volume="0">
> ```
>
> *No user controller is displayed.*

ActiveX

WHAT IS THIS?

ActiveX is a programming language from Microsoft that makes it possible to call up more complex applications. ActiveX is a competitor of Java.

ActiveX control elements are only displayed in Internet Explorer under Windows. It does not run on Macintosh and is not interpreted by Netscape Navigator.

1 In the document window, click where you want to insert the control element.

2 Click on the button in the Object manager on the SPECIAL panel. ActiveX is inserted as a dummy in the document.

3 Mark the dummy and set the integrated media file in the Property Inspector.

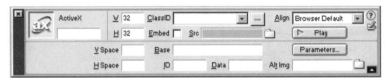

4 Activate the EMBED check box if the element is to be shown in Netscape.

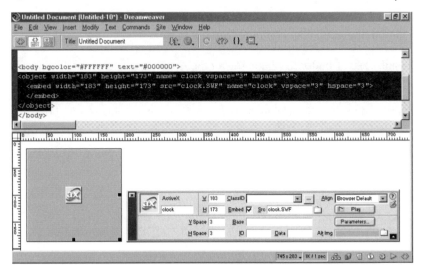

Java Applets

Java Applets are small programs which are embedded in the Web page.

> **WHAT IS THIS?**
>
> **Java** is an object-oriented, platform-comprehensive programming language, developed by Sun Microsystems and based on C++.

How to insert a Java Applet on the Web page:

1 In the document window, click where the Applet should appear.

2 Click on the Applet button 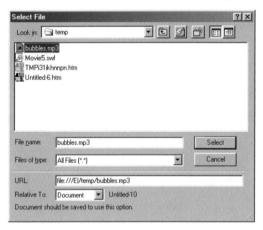 in the Object manager (SPECIAL panel). Or select INSERT/MEDIA/APPLET. The SELECT FILE dialog box appears.

3 Look for the Applet on your computer and select it.

4 Click on the SELECT button. The dummy for the Applet appears in the document window.

5 Select the dummy and determine the parameters of the Java Applets in the Property Inspector.

CAUTION

The BASE box in the Property Inspector is automatically filled in. For browsers that are not Java capable, you can put in an alternative image.

Chapter 12

Publishing Web sites

When you have completed your Web pages, you will probably want to publish them. Dreamweaver is all you need to show them to the world. It doesn't matter whether you want to publish the Web page on an Intranet or on the World Wide Web. In this last workshop you will see how simple it is.

The site window is not only a file manager, it can also function as an integrated FTP client in Dreamweaver. You can put your files onto the Web quickly and simply with this. With this tool, you can also download files from the Web.

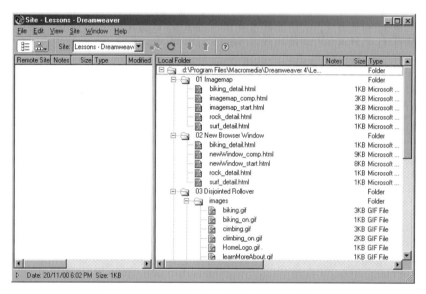

WHAT IS THIS?

The **File Transfer Protocol** (**FTP**) is a standardised procedure for transferring files in the network.

By default, the right of the site window shows the local files and directories (see Altering site settings on page 296). In Dreamweaver, you can modify some site settings for windows. The remote site is shown on the left half.

WHAT IS THIS?

The **remote site** is the files and directories which are installed on a remote server and which can be accessed by several people.

Setting up the remote site

First, set up a local site. You learnt how to do this in Chapter 2, Local site and project management.

Next, you need to decide in which server the site should be located. Ask your system administrator, or your customers, about the names of servers and what you should pay attention to when transmitting the data. Get hold of the submission data (login and password).

> **TIPS**
>
> • *The structure of your local directories should correspond to the remote Web site. In practice, Dreamweaver duplicates the local structure if you want to upload your site or just parts of it.*
>
> • *Test your site before you make it available to the public. Only when you are sure that it does not contain any errors should you copy it onto the server.*

How to define an FTP connection to a Web server:

1 Select DEFINE SITES from the SITE drop-down menu in the site window.

Or select SITE/DEFINE SITES in the menu bar of the site window.

2 Select an existing site from the DEFINE SITES dialog box and click on EDIT.

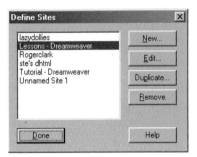

3 Click on REMOTE INFORMATION in the category box in the SITE DEFINITION dialog window.

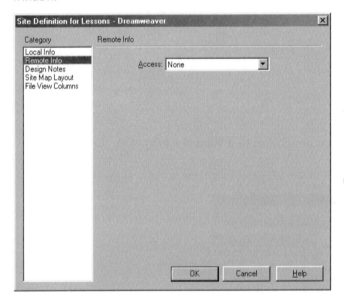

4 Select one of the following access options:

- Select NONE if you do not wish to publish your site on a server.

- If the Web server is set up within a network, or if this is run on your local computer, click on LOCAL/NETWORK. Click on the folder icon or name the directory directly where the Web site should be placed.

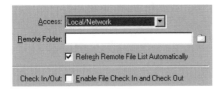

5 Activate the REFRESH REMOTE FILE LIST AUTOMATICALLY check box if the remote site is to be refreshed automatically, in case you have made changes to the local site.

NOTE

If you want to refresh the remote site manually, select VIEW/REFRESH or press F5 *in the site window.*

6 Select the FTP entry if your Web server supports this protocol.

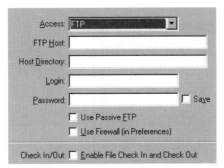

- Enter the FTP host names in the FTP HOST box. This is the whole Internet name of a computer system, such as, for example, `ftp.intermedia.net`.

- Enter the host directory where the page should be located. All users can access this directory and the documents within this. Thereby, the files in this are accessible to the public.

- Enter the login names (LOGIN) and PASSWORD in the other text boxes. Activate the SAVE check box so that you do not need to enter a new password every time.

- A firewall must be considered when connecting to the remote server. Activate the USE FIREWALL check box. Some firewalls require a passive FTP. The connection is then established from the local site, instead of from a remote site.

WHAT IS THIS?

*A **firewall** is a piece of security software used to separate the internal operational net (Intranet) from the external Internet.*

You can obtain further useful information from your system administrator.

7 Click on the OK button to confirm your entries.

> **CAUTION**
>
> *Use the same directory structure on the remote server as on your local computer. Then you can be sure that the links and images are correct and are displayed.*

Altering site settings

In Dreamweaver, you can alter some settings for the site window.

1 Open the PREFERENCES window using EDIT/PREFERENCES in the menu bar. When the dialog box opens, it already has the FTP setting.

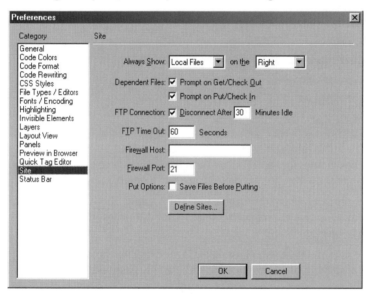

2 By default, Dreamweaver displays the local files on the right and removed documents on the left side of the site window. If you prefer another setting, set this with the corresponding drop-down menu. This setting also affects the representation of the site map in the site window.

3 If a dialog box will be shown with the subordinate files, activate the check boxes. The dialog box appears during the checking in and/or checking out.

4 Increase or decrease the default disconnection of the FTP connection after 30 minutes of laying idle, if you have direct access to the network, the automatic connection should be deactivated.

Making a connection with a remote site

To up or download a file from a remote site, you will first need to make a connection with this setting.

1 Select the remote site you want to connect to.

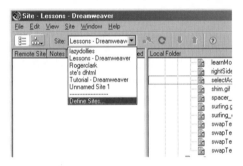

2 Click on the CONNECT TO REMOTE HOST  button. Or, in the menu bar of the site window, choose SITE/CONNECT or press [Ctrl] + [Alt] + [⇧] + [F5].

For the connection, Dreamweaver uses the information that you have entered during the definition of the remote site.

The ESTABLISH CONNECTION WITH [HOST NAME] dialog window appears.

If you have successfully connected to the Web server, the CONNECT button changes into the DISCONNECT button.

The files on the Web server appear.

How to sever the connection with the remote server:

1 Make sure that no more files are being transferred. To do this, check the status bar. CONNECT TO [SITE NAME] should stand here.

2 Click on the CONNECT TO REMOTE HOST button in the site window.

> **CAUTION**
>
> *If it takes longer than 30 minutes to transfer data, Dreamweaver will sever the connection. You can change this value in the settings.*

Uploading files

If the connection is set up, you can upload files from your local site to the remote server.

> **NOTE**
>
> *If you put the files in a directory that does not exist on the remote site, Dreamweaver will automatically create it.*

1 Select the file and the directory that you would like to upload in the site window.

2 Click on PUT.

Or select SITE/PUT in the site window, or press [Ctrl] + [⇧] + [U].

Alternatively, click on the PUT FILES [⬆] button.

The DEPENDENT FILES dialog box appears.

WHAT IS THIS?

Dependent files are images, animations, style sheets and other files that are connected to the HTML document. If the browser loads the HTML document, all of the dependent files will also be called.

---

3 Click on YES or NO.

4 You can follow the progress of the uploads in the status bar.

Downloading files

Working the other way around, you can also copy files and directories from the remote server onto your local hard drive.

1 Make sure that the connection is established.

2 Select the files you would like to download in the site window.

3 Click on the GET FILES [⬇] button. Or, select SITE/GET from the menu bar in the site window, or press [Ctrl] + [⇧] + [D].

4 You can follow the progress of the download in the status bar.

Synchronisation

Dreamweaver can search a directory, or a whole site, for newer files, and then copy these on to the remote server or the local computer.

1 Open the local site in the site window.

2 Establish the connection with the corresponding remote server.

3 Depending on which files you want to coordinate, select EDIT/SELECT NEWER LOCAL or EDIT/SELECT NEWER REMOTE in the menu bar of the site window.

4 If Dreamweaver has completed the coordination, the newer files will be displayed behind. You can call these files with a double click (see Downloading files on page 299), put them on standby (see Uploading files on page 298) or synchronise them.

5 Select SITE/SYNCHRONIZE from the menu bar in the site window. The SYNCHRONIZE FILES dialog window appears.

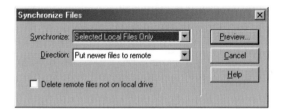

6 In SYNCHRONIZE from the drop-down menu, select whether you would like to synchronise the whole site or only certain files.

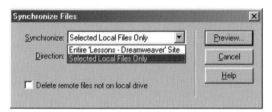

7 In the second drop-down menu, you determine the DIRECTION. Here you can determine whether you want to call the files and directories, put them on standby, or synchronise in both directions.

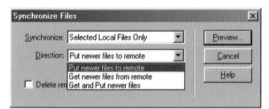

8 Click on the PREVIEW button. The SITE dialog box appears.

9 Click on OK to upload or download the files entered. Follow the process in the status bar.

Refreshing the view

If you have uploaded and downloaded files and directories from the local computer onto the remote server, the view in the site window may not be up to date any more. To be sure that it reflects the latest state, you can refresh the view.

- Select VIEW/REFRESH from the menu bar in the site window or press $\boxed{\text{F5}}$ or click on the $\boxed{\text{C}}$ button. Both the local and the remote Web site views are refreshed.

- To refresh only the local site view, you need to select VIEW/REFRESH LOCAL or press $\boxed{\Uparrow}$ + $\boxed{\text{F5}}$.

- If you want to refresh the view of the remote site, select VIEW/REFRESH REMOTE or press $\boxed{\text{Alt}}$ + $\boxed{\text{F5}}$.

Appendix

Questions and answers

Every time I try to open a window, nothing happens. The launcher is open, but where has the window gone?

Select WINDOW/ARRANGE PANELS in the menu bar.

It is possible to call up the document and the site window with the icons in the status bar. All other windows are floating windows, which are called panels and inspectors.

How does Fireworks cooperate with Dreamweaver?

You can open and edit Fireworks graphics directly in Dreamweaver. Double click on the graphic to start Fireworks. If this does not work, check the entry in the PREFERENCES (EDIT/PREFERENCES) in the FILE TYPES/EDITORS category. Here Fireworks needs to use the .gif, .jpg or .png extensions.

Do the objects and behaviours that I created in previous Dreamweaver versions work?

Yes. Dreamweaver 4 is downward compatible.

I have put a link within the same document, but it doesn't work. What have I done wrong?

Named anchors consist of two parts. Check whether you have set links and labels (see Chapter 5).

Is it possible to create a database application in Dreamweaver?

You cannot create any database connections with Dreamweaver 4. APS, JSP or ColdFusion applications can be developed with Dreamweaver UltraDev. This program is based on Dreamweaver 4.

I have drawn a table in the layout mode, but can I insert any content?

You can only edit the cells with content in the layout mode. Dreamweaver has therefore inserted a protective blank space in the newly inserted cells. All the other cells (without any content) will not be editable in the layout mode to begin with, unless you have created these with the INSERT CELLS tool.

You will need to be in the standard mode if you want to insert content in an empty table cell.

In the layout mode, tables and cells can only be inserted in cells where there is no content.

Glossary and important shortcuts

A

ActiveX Programming language from Microsoft that makes complex applications possible, which you can call up with a browser. ActiveX is a competitor of Java.

B

Browser Internet program, such as Internet Explorer, Netscape.

C

Cascading Style Sheet "Progressive gradeable format template"; HTML expansion that allows a more exact layout of the Web page.

CGI "Common Gateway Interface"; software interface for Internet servers to transfer parameters to programs and scripts from the server for the processing of information (from forms); CGI scripts are written, for example, in Perl, C++, Java or JavaScript.

Child tag HTML command enclosed in another (parent) tag.

Clients Intelligent terminals within a network structure that transfer tasks to one or several central servers, gather them and then process them for the user.

Content frame Contents window for a Web page.

CSS see Cascading Style Sheet.

Cursor Blinking bar that displays the insertion position for text, images and other elements.

D

Debugger Software that searches code for errors and solves them.

DHTML Based on JavaScript, CSS and HTML; Dynamic HTML is interpreted by Netscape Version 4.0 and later, MS Internet Explorer from version 4.0. Netscape and Internet Explorer interpret these commands quite differently.

Download Downloading of Web pages, documents, images, animations, sound files and similar. A remote server is accessed in the process.

Drop-down menu A menu that opens with a mouse click. It contains several selectable options and settings. Depending on whether such a menu opens upwards or downwards, it is called a pop-up or drop-down menu.

Dynamic HTML see DHTML.

F

File Gathering of information saved in a storage medium under a specified name.

Firewall Security software used to separate the internal Intranet from the external Internet.

Frame

- Frames consist of two parts: a frameset, and a content document, which is the actual frame. The **frameset** is an HTML page, whose structures of visible documents (frames) are fixed to each other. A frame is therefore an HTML document. In the frameset, it is defined which documents should be displayed and where they should be placed, in what size. The frameset is a kind of control instance that moves in the background and holds the documents together. The frameset is also described as a **"superior frame",** and a frame as a **"subordinate frameX".**

- A scene of an animation; frames and **key frames** are represented by small boxes in the timeline.

FTP The "File Transfer Protocol" is a standardised procedure used to transfer files in the network.

G

GIF The **image** format from CompuServe that can save up to 256 colours. Areas of an image can be saved transparently.

305

H

Headline Heading.

Homepage Entry page of an Internet or Intranet display. It appears when you call an address (URL).

Host Name for a server in a network.

Hotspot see Imagemap.

HTML Hyper Text Markup Language; the leading language on the Web. Document description language that supports hyperlinks.

Hyperlink *(Link)* Reference from a Web site to other documents, definite text areas, or to an e-mail address.

Hyper Text Markup Language see HTML.

I

Icon Symbol.

IE Internet Explorer.

Imagemap An image split into individual parts (hotspots). These hotspots are linked to various pages.

Intranet A closed network working as a small independent Internet. Usually it is connected to the Internet and secured with firewalls.

J

Java Object-oriented, platform-comprehensive programming language, developed by Sun Microsystems and based on C++.

Java Applet Small Java program for use in Internet programs.

JavaScript Script language interpreted and run by browsers. Interactive elements of a Web page can be programmed in JavaScript. The Behaviour Inspector in Dreamweaver inserts JavaScript automatically in the source code.

JPG, JPEG Image format that supports millions of colours and therefore achieves good detail presentation. However, colour information is lost during compression. The more you compress a JPG, the smaller its file size, but at the same time the more colours are lost. The image loses sharpness and becomes pixelated.

K

Kbps "Kilobytes per second"; measurement unit for the transfer rate.

Key frame A frame assigned with certain properties. These properties are applied to neighbouring frames in a modified form. Through this, you get fluent transitions between the individual key frames.

L

Layer Container on the Web page which can hold content and be placed wherever you desire. Layers are part of Cascading Style Sheets (CSS) and Dynamic HTML (DHTML). They are laid out three-dimensionally: you can place them on the X and Y axis both as absolute and relative values. The Z axis allows the stacking of several layers.

Link see Hyperlink.

Logo Trademarks, word/image brand of a company.

M

Mouse over see Rollover.

N

NN Netscape Navigator.

P

Parent tag Superior HTML control command.

Plugin Additional module of a software, installed directly into the interface. For example, Flash animations can only be played if the Flash plugin is installed on the browser.

PNG Image format that supports index colours, grey scale, true colour images and alpha channels. There is no loss of quality when compressing: there are no limitations to the number of colours. At the moment, only a few browsers (among others IE and NN from version 4) can interpret it.

Pop-up menu see Drop-down menu.

R

Remote site Files and directories that are installed on a remote server and can be accessed by a number of people.

Rollover Image that changes if you move the mouse pointer over it. A rollover consists of two images: the primary image (this image is shown when the page is loaded) and the rollover image.

S

Scaling To alter the height and/or width of an image or another page element.

Scroll Moving a document up or down with the arrow buttons or the slide (scrollbar) on the right border.

Shortcut(s) Keyboard shortcut(s), such as [Ctrl], [S].

Site(s) see Web site.

Site root Site directory.

Sound Audio files/sound documents.

T

Tag Start and end HTML command that encloses the formatting document area, such as **This text is written in bold.**

Template Layout pattern for several Web pages; contains locked and editable elements.

Third party Stands for any other source (mostly companies) that offers additions, complements, etc. for the program of another company.

U

Upload Files and directories uploaded or copied from a remote computer (remote server).

URL "Uniform Resource Locator". Internet address format, according to whose default format all Internet addresses must be constructed (location: //Server/Domain.TopLevelDomain/Directory/File); e.g. http://www.intermedia.net/dreamweaver/content.htm

User Anyone who surfs on the Internet. A user is a visitor to your Web page.

W

Web Abbreviation for World Wide Web; see also WWW.

Web page A single HTML page.

Web site All Web pages of an Internet appearance; can consist of more than a hundred documents that are linked to each other.

WWW World Wide Web; multimedia service on the Internet. Distributed hypertext information system on client/server architecture, through HTTP protocol.

WYSIWYG "What You See Is What You Get"; editor with a graphical user interface. What you create and see in the program will also be displayed on the Web site. However, there may well be differences between individual browsers.

The most important keyboard shortcuts for Windows

(see also inside cover)

Page views

Action	Keyboard shortcuts
Standard view	`Ctrl` + `⇧` + `F6`
Layout view	`Ctrl` + `F6`
Symbol bar	`Ctrl` + `⇧` + `T`

Displaying page elements

Action	Keyboard shortcuts
Visual aids	`Ctrl` + `⇧` + `I`
Rulers	`Ctrl` + `Alt` + `R`
Show grid	`Ctrl` + `Alt` + `G`
Snap to grid	`Ctrl` + `Alt` + `⇧` + `G`
Head content	`Ctrl` + `⇧` + `W`
Page properties	`Ctrl` + `⇧` + `J`

Editing text

Action	Keyboard shortcuts
Create new paragraph	`↵`
Insert line break 	`⇧` + `↵`
Insert protected blank space	`Ctrl` + `⇧` + `⎵`

309

Action	Keyboard shortcuts
Move text or object to somewhere else on the page	Pull the selected element to the desired position
Copy text or object to somewhere else on the page	Pull the selected element to the new position while pressing the `Ctrl` key
Select a word	Double click on the word
Add selected elements to the library	`Ctrl` + `⇧` + `B`
Switch between the design view and the code editor	`Ctrl` + `⇥`
Open and close the Property Inspector	`Ctrl` + `⇧` + `J`
Check spelling	`Ctrl` + `F7`

Formatting text

Action	Keyboard shortcuts
Indent	`Ctrl` + `9`
Outdent	`Ctrl` + `8`
Format / None	`Ctrl` + `0`
Paragraph format	`Ctrl` + `⇧` + `P`
Headings 1 to 6 used on the paragraph	`Ctrl` + `1` to `6`
Align / Left	`Ctrl` + `⇧` + `Alt` + `L`
Align / Centre	`Ctrl` + `⇧` + `Alt` + `C`
Align / Right	`Ctrl` + `⇧` + `Alt` + `R`
Display selected text in bold	`Ctrl` + `B`
Display selected text in italics	`Ctrl` + `I`
Edit style sheet	`Ctrl` + `⇧` + `E`
Search	`Ctrl` + `F`
Search further/New search	`F3`

Action	Keyboard shortcuts
Replace	Ctrl + H

Working with tables

Action	Keyboard shortcuts
Select table (cursor placed within the table)	Ctrl + A
Jump to the next cell	Tab
Jump to the previous cell	⇧ + Tab
Insert row (above the current row)	Ctrl + M
Insert row at the end of the table	Tab in the last cell
Delete the current cell	Ctrl + ⇧ + M
Insert column	Ctrl + ⇧ + A
Delete column	Ctrl + ⇧ + -
Connect selected table cells	Ctrl + Alt + M
Separate table cells	Ctrl + Alt + S
Refresh table layout	Ctrl + ⎵

Working with templates

Action	Keyboard shortcuts
Create new editable regions	Ctrl + Alt + V

311

Working with frames

Action	Keyboard shortcuts
Select frame	Click on the frame with a depressed [Alt] key
Select next frame or next frameset	[Alt] + [→]
Select previous frame or previous frameset	[Alt] + [←]
Select the superior frameset	[Alt] + [↑]
Select the first sub frame or the first sub frameset	[Alt] + [↓]
Insert new frame in frameset	Drag the frame border while pressing the [Alt] key
Insert a new frame in the frameset with the drag method	Drag the frame border while pressing the [Alt] and [Ctrl] key

Working with layers

Action	Keyboard shortcuts
Select layer	Click while pressing [Ctrl] + [⇧]
Select and move layer	Move while pressing [Ctrl] + [⇧]
Insert layer in selection or remove layer from the selection	Click on the layer while pressing [⇧]
Move selected layer in pixel steps	Arrow keys
Move selected layer in grid increments	[⇧] + arrow keys
Enlarge or reduce selected layers in pixel steps	[Ctrl] + arrow keys
Enlarge or reduce selected layers in grid increments	[Ctrl] + [⇧] + arrow keys
Align the last selected layer with the upper/bottom/left/right edge	[Ctrl] + [↑] / [↓] / [←] / [→]

Action	Keyboard shortcuts
Set the same width for the selected layers	Ctrl + ⇧ + I
Set the same height for the selected layers	Ctrl + ⇧ + I
Activating/deactivating preferences for the nesting of layers	Ctrl + drag
Show/hide grid	Ctrl + ⇧ + Alt + G
Align to grid	Ctrl + Alt + G

Working with the timeline

Action	Keyboard shortcuts
Insert object in the timeline	Ctrl + Alt + ⇧ + T
Add key frame	⇧ + F9
Remove key frame	Del

Working with images

Action	Keyboard shortcuts
Change the image source attribute	Double click on the image
Edit an image in an external editor	Double click on the image while pressing the Ctrl key

Calling help

Action	Keyboard shortcuts
Using help topics	F1
Reference	⇧ + F1
Support Centre	Ctrl + F1

Managing hyperlinks

Action	Keyboard shortcuts
Create link (select text)	Ctrl + L
Remove link	Ctrl + ⇧ + L
Drag and drop to create a link from a document	Select text, images or object and drag the selection with a pressed ⇧ key to a file in the site window
Drag and drop to create a link in the Property Inspector	Select text, image or object and then drag the file pointer from the Property Inspector to a file in the site window
Open connected document in Dreamweaver	Double click on the link while pressing the Ctrl key
Check selected links	⇧ + F8
Check all links in the site	Ctrl + F8

Target browsers and previewing in browsers

Action	Keyboard shortcuts
Preview in primary browser	F12
Preview in secondary browser	Ctrl + F12

Debugging browsers

Action	Keyboard shortcuts
Debug in the primary browser	Alt + F12
Debug in the secondary browser	Ctrl + Alt + F12

Site management and FTP

Action	Keyboard shortcuts (shift)
Create new file	[Ctrl] + [⇧] + [N]
Create a new directory	[Ctrl] + [⇧] + [Alt] + [N]
Open selection	[Ctrl] + [⇧] + [Alt] + [O]
Call up selected files or directories from a remote FTP site	[Ctrl] + [⇧] + [D] or drag the files in the site window from the area in the remote files to the local area
Provide selected files or directories on the remote FTP site	[Ctrl] + [⇧] + [U] or drag the files in the site window from the local file area to the remote area
Check out	[Ctrl] + [⇧] + [Alt] + [D]
Check in	[Ctrl] + [⇧] + [Alt] + [U]
Display site map	[Alt] + [F8]
Refresh remote site	[Alt] + [F5]

History panel

Action	Keyboard shortcuts
Open history panel	[⇧] + [F10]
Start/stop command recording	[Ctrl] + [⇧] + [X]
Play recorded command	[Ctrl] + [P]

Site map

Action	Keyboard shortcuts
View site files	[F8]
Refresh local display area	[⇧] + [F5]
Define as site root	[Ctrl] + [R]

315

Action	Keyboard shortcuts
Create link to existing file	Ctrl + ⇧ + K
Alter link	Ctrl + L
Remove link	Del
Display/remove link	Ctrl + ⇧ + Y
Display page title	Ctrl + ⇧ + T
Name file	F2
Enlarge site map	Ctrl + + (plus character)
Reduce site map	Ctrl + - (minus character)

Playing plugins

Action	Keyboard shortcuts
Play plugin	Ctrl + Alt + P
Stop plugin	Ctrl + Alt + X
Play all plugins	Ctrl + ⇧ + Alt + P
Stop all plugins	Ctrl + ⇧ + Alt + X

Inserting objects

Action	Keyboard shortcuts
Desired object (image, Shockwave movie, etc.)	Drag file from Explorer or the site window into the document window
Image	Ctrl + Alt + I
Table	Ctrl + Alt + T
Flash movie	Ctrl + Alt + F
Shockwave Director movie	Ctrl + Alt + D
Named anchor	Ctrl + Alt + A

Opening and closing panels

Action	Keyboard shortcuts
Object	`Ctrl` + `F2`
Properties	`Ctrl` + `F3`
Site files	`F5`
Site map	`Ctrl` + `F5`
Elements	`F11`
CSS styles	`⇧` + `F11`
HTML styles	`Ctrl` + `F11`
Behaviour	`⇧` + `F3`
History	`⇧` + `F10`
Timeline	`⇧` + `F9`
Code Inspector	`F10`
Frames	`⇧` + `F2`
Layers	`F2`
Reference	`Ctrl` + `⇧` + `F1`
Hide and show floating panels	`F4`
Reduce all windows	`⇧` + `F4`
Restore all windows	`Alt` + `⇧` + `F4`

Special characters (a selection)

Character	Description	Name in HTML	Unicode in HTML
	forced non breaking space	` `	` `
¡	inverted exclamation mark	`&iexcl;`	`&#161;`
¿	inverted question mark	`&iquest;`	`&#191;`

317

Character	Description	Name in HTML	Unicode in HTML
¶	Paragraph	&para;	&#182;
–	Dash width n	&ndash;	&#8211;
—	Dash width m	&mdash;	&#8212;
'	single left quotation mark	&lsquo;	&#8216;
'	single right quotation mark	&rsquo;	&#8217;
"	double left quotation mark	&ldquo;	&#8220;
"	double right quotation mark	&rdquo;	&#8221;
«	left bended quotation mark	&laquo;	&#171;
»	right bended quotation mark	&raquo;	&#187;

Currencies

Character	Description	Name in HTML	Unicode in HTML
¢	Cent	&cent;	&#162;
£	Pound character	&pound;	&#163;
¥	Yen character	&yen;	&#165;

Business

Character	Description	Name in HTML	Unicode in HTML
©	Copyright	&copy;	&#169;
®	Registered	&reg;	&#174;
™	Trademark	&trade;	&#8482;

Mathematics

Character	Description	Name in HTML	Unicode in HTML
±	Plus minus character	&plusmn;	&#177;
÷	Division character	&divide;	&#247;
¢	Minutes character	&prime;	&#8242;
‾	Over score	&oline;	&#8254;
/	Fraction line	&frasl;	&#8260;
∂	partial	&part;	&#8706;
∏	product	&prod;	&#8719;
²	sum	&sum;	&#8721;
–	minus	&minus;	&#8722;

Measurements

Character	Description	Name in HTML	Unicode in HTML
µ	Micro character	&micro;	&#181;
°	Degree character	&deg;	&#176;

Arrows

Character	Description	Name in HTML	Unicode in HTML
←	left arrow	&larr;	&#8592;
↑	arrow up	&uarr;	&#8593;
→	right arrow	&rarr;	&#8594;
↓	arrow down	&darr;	&#8595;
↔	left/right arrow	&harr;	&#8596;

Internet protocols

For absolute hyperlink entries you will have to enter the corresponding protocol type. These protocols accomplish various tasks:

http://	Hyper Text Transfer Protocol
gopher://	Gopher Hypertext Index
shttp://	Secure Hyper Text Transfer Protocol (used by servers in the secure area)
ftp://	File Transfer Protocol
mailto:	Internet E-Mail Address
news:	Usenet, discussion forum or another network
telnet:	Teletype Network, allows the remote control of a remote computer
wais://	Wide Area Internet Search

Common top level domains

.com	commercial organisation
.edu	educational institution
.gov	US government
.mil	US military
.net	network provider
.org	non profit organisation
.au	Austria
.ca	Canada
.ch	Switzerland
.cn	China
.de	Germany
.dk	Denmark
.ed	Spain
.fi	Finland

.fr	France
.it	Italy
.jp	Japan
.kr	South Korea
.mx	Mexico
.my	Malaysia
.nl	Netherlands
.nz	New Zealand
.se	Sweden
.sg	Singapore
.tw	Taiwan
.uk	United Kingdom
.us	United States
.za	South Africa

Surf tips: interesting hyperlinks

Sun Microsystems Inc.: JavaServer Pages (JSP)

```
http://java.sun.com/products/jsp/
```

Scriptsearch

```
http://scriptsearch.internet.com/pages/14.shtml
```

ActiveX

```
www.microsoft.com
```

Dreamweaver downloads/Macromedia Exchange

```
www.macromedia.com
```

HTML and Web technologies

World Wide Web Consortium: Descriptions of Web technology, guidelines, software and tools.

```
http://www.w3.org
```

O'Reilly Open Source Software Convention

```
http://conferences.oreilly.com/oscon2001
```

CGI Resources

```
http://www.cgi-resources.com
```

The Common Gateway Interface

```
http://hoohoo.ncsa.uiuc.edu/cgi
```

XML (O'Reilly & Associates, Inc.)

```
www.xml.com
```

Cascading Style Sheets specifications (CSS1)

W3C: Recommendations

```
http://www.w3.org/TR/REC-CSS1
```

Dynamic HTML (DHTML)

Macromedia: Tutorial

```
http://www.dhtmlzone.com/index.html
```

DHTML Workshop

```
http://msdn.microsoft.com/default.asp?url=/workshop/author/
dhtml/dhtml.asp
```

Java Applets, JavaScript, Perl and other scripts

Matt's Script Archive: CGI/Perls to download

```
http://www.worldwidemart.com/scripts
```

Sun Microsystems Inc.: Java Tutorial, XML, etc.

```
www.javasoft.com
```

Javaboutique: Info and Applets to download

```
http://javaboutique.internet.com
```

Javaside: Applets to download

```
www.javaside.com
```

Hotwired Webmonkey: Perl, CGI scripts

```
http://www.hotwired.com/webmonkey/99/26/
index4a.html?tw=programming
```

Database

Hypertext Preprocessor PHP

```
http://www.php.net
```

Microsoft: Active Server Pages (ASP)

```
http://msdn.microsoft.com/workshop/server/asp/ASPover.asp
```

Online magazine

ZDNet

```
www.zdnet.com
```

323

Web site promotion – the most important English search engines

```
http://www.yahoo.co.uk
http://www.altavista.co.uk
http://www.lycos.co.uk
http://www.infoseek.co.uk
http://www.excite.co.uk
http://www.google.co.uk
http://www.hotbot.co.uk
http://www.ukindex.co.uk
http://www.ukplus.co.uk
http://www.ukdirectory.com
http://www.eblast.com
http://www.searchuk.com
```

Index

329